WAR WITHOUT RULES

WAR WITHOUT RULES

★

CHINA'S PLAYBOOK FOR GLOBAL DOMINATION

Brigadier General
Robert Spalding

(US Air Force, Retired)

SENTINEL

Sentinel
An imprint of Penguin Random House LLC
penguinrandomhouse.com

Most Sentinel books are available at a discount when purchased in quantity for sales promotions or corporate use. Special editions, which include personalized covers, excerpts, and corporate imprints, can be created when purchased in large quantities. For more information, please call (212) 572-2232 or email specialmarkets@penguinrandomhouse.com. Your local bookstore can also assist with discounted bulk purchases using the Penguin Random House corporate Business-to-Business program. For assistance in locating a participating retailer, email B2B@penguinrandomhouse.com.

LIBRARY OF CONGRESS CATALOGING-IN-PUBLICATION DATA
Names: Spalding, Robert S., III, 1966– author.
Title: War without rules : China's playbook for global domination / Robert Spalding.
Other titles: China's playbook for global domination
Description: New York : Sentinel, [2022]
Identifiers: LCCN 2021058186 (print) | LCCN 2021058187 (ebook) |
ISBN 9780593331040 (hardcover) | ISBN 9780593331057 (ebook)
Subjects: LCSH: China—Military policy—History—
21st century. | United States—Foreign relations—China. |
China—Foreign relations—United States. | Hybrid warfare—China.
Classification: LCC UA835 .S65 2022 (print) | LCC UA835 (ebook) |
DDC 355/.033251—dc23/eng/20220112
LC record available at https://lccn.loc.gov/2021058186
LC ebook record available at https://lccn.loc.gov/2021058187

Printed in the United States of America
1   3   5   7   9   10   8   6   4   2

Book design by Daniel Lagin

For Steph

If history teaches anything, it teaches that simple-minded appeasement or wishful thinking about our adversaries is folly.

It means the betrayal of our past, the squandering of our freedom.

We know only too well that war comes not when the forces of freedom are strong, but when they are weak. It is then that tyrants are tempted.

—Ronald Reagan

All warfare is based on deception.

—Sun Tzu

CONTENTS

INTRODUCTION

WHEN I FIRST READ THE CHINESE WAR MANUAL *UNRE-stricted Warfare* in 1999, I thought it was wacky. I was flying B-2 stealth bombers out of Whiteman Air Force Base in western Missouri and reading a lot about war. As an Air Force officer, I thought it was part of my day job to understand the bigger picture—even though the prevailing attitude in the military was "Just fly the planes." *UW* was one of those books that caused a stir among some military folks because it had recently been translated into English. It had that insider whiff of mystery and secrets, a peek into the mind of the Chinese Communist Party.

Despite that mystique, not a lot of people were finishing the book. For one thing, regardless of its title, no one thought we were ever going to be fighting a war with China, so it seemed like a lot of work for very little payoff. For another, the book itself is not a light read. It is a dense compendium of strategy, economics, social theory, and futuristic thoughts about technology. It imparts centuries of military history, particularly as it relates to the United States, but I already knew a lot of that. It seemed vague and also a little sci-fi, not relevant to a U.S. bomber pilot—even one with a fascination for military history. My mistake.

If you look closely at everything China has done since 1999—at all aspects of its economic, military, diplomatic, and technological relations with the rest of the world—it's like watching *Unrestricted Warfare* come to life. One can find other glimpses into the secretive mentality of the CCP leaders, but this one is the single most important book for understanding the China of today. *Unrestricted Warfare* is the main blueprint for China's efforts to unseat America as the world's economic, political, and ideological leader. It shows exactly how a totalitarian nation set out to dominate the West through a comprehensive, long-term strategy that includes everything from corporate sabotage to cyberwarfare to dishonest diplomacy; from violations of international trade law and intellectual property law to calculated abuses of the global financial system. As one of the authors stated, "The only rule in *Unrestricted Warfare* is that there are no rules."

The book is the key to decoding China's master plan for world domination, which has been progressing more steadily and successfully than most Americans realize—even accelerating in the reign of Xi Jinping. Manipulating COVID policies, stonewalling the world about its origins, and mounting a massive disinformation campaign to blame the United States are merely recent examples.

So why is *Unrestricted Warfare* so obscure, even to people who study China professionally on behalf of the U.S. government, the Fortune 500, the investment world, the nonprofit world, academia, or the military? It's not as if the book is some secret document that has never escaped the inner sanctum of the Chinese Communist

Party. Just the opposite: The original translation by the U.S. government is in the public domain; you can google it and click on an English translation, for free, in less than a second.

The problem is that *Unrestricted Warfare* is hard to read. While any American can access it, few can understand it. The prose is dense and confusing, even in the original Mandarin, and even more so in that crude, free translation you'll find on the web. Its insights are clouded by endless repetitions and meandering discursions into military history, cultural theory, and attacks on U.S. policy. The colonels, Qiao Liang and Wang Xiangsui, get tangled in semantics and draw on faulty citations and unsourced references. They obsess about the Persian Gulf War of 1990–91 to an extent that puzzles Americans who consider that war to be a minor footnote to history. And the authors' metaphors are so weird to our ears as to seem utterly baffling. Just consider two chapter titles: "The War God's Face Has Become Indistinct" and "What Do Americans Gain by Touching the Elephant?" Huh?

I mentioned *Unrestricted Warfare* several times in my previous book, *Stealth War: How China Took Over While America's Elite Slept.* I noted that the book was well-known to modern-day China scholars but that perhaps because of its strange complexity, Western analysts had failed to connect its strategic vision with the seemingly random actions of China's misleadingly benign and smiling countenance. Although some of the text is pretty clear: "Using all means, including armed force or non-armed force, military and non-military, and lethal and non-lethal means to compel the enemy to accept one's interest."

As I wrote at the time, that strategy can justify meddling in all manner of another country's affairs: silencing ideas or promoting political discord, stealing technology, dumping products to disrupt markets. I was intrigued with the idea of creating an "army" of academics who could be used to gather medical, technological, and engineering information. The list of incursions goes on—and has grown since then.

Consider just a small number of the things the Chinese Communists have done:

- Seized on COVID as a weapon to be used to their benefit, not a humanitarian crisis to be solved.
- Viewed the climate change issue as a bargaining chip to win them economic concessions from global elites in return for reforms that they never intend to make.
- Sponsored corporate espionage on a scale beyond what the United States acknowledges.
- Launched unrelenting cyberattacks against Western companies and governments.
- Fueled America's deadly fentanyl drug crisis by allowing illegal smuggling of banned substances.
- Used slave labor to produce goods such as clothing for sale to Western shoppers.

Despite all of these actions by the CCP, since publication of *Stealth War,* I've encountered skepticism from some readers who simply can't believe that China has been methodically undermining the rest of the world with a patient, long-term, multidisciplinary strategy. Some even dismissed *Stealth War* as the work of an alarmist.

In the wake of that reaction, I realized how useful it would be to make the Chinese manual of war accessible to American readers so that they can see it for themselves. I set out to write a user-friendly guide that would explain *UW* chapter by chapter, adding examples while editing out the irrelevant and distracting parts of the original text. In the process I've drawn on history, military strategy, and Chinese culture to explain the context in which *Unrestricted Warfare* was written and then applied. My goal is to show how *UW*'s advice to the leadership of the CCP maps with terrifying consistency onto the events of the past two decades.

This book has opened my eyes to how the CCP has essentially sneak attacked us in slow motion. And made me think hard about where they are going next. I hope it can have the same effect on others. I want to share with the men and women in our government, my respected former colleagues, who have to make some important—maybe life and death—decisions about how we deal with the Chinese government in the very near future.

I know it can seem excessive to compare any country with Nazi Germany. But as we rethink our views on China, what other comparison is appropriate for a regime that casually and cold-bloodedly allowed COVID-19 to spread to the rest of the world at the same time it was forcing its Muslim citizens into concentration camps? Hong Kong parallels the takeover of Austria in 1938. And how do you account for the increasingly warlike rhetoric and military movements directed at Taiwan?

Imagine the reaction during World War II if an American company had tried to export its goods to imperial Japan, or if a Wall Street firm had tried to underwrite the bonds of a Nazi arms manufacturer.

Unthinkable, right? And yet today countless Americans are still trying to do business with and in China, misunderstanding or ignoring the CCP's war without rules.

I am deeply concerned that the Biden administration, despite some positive moves, is seriously underestimating the malevolence and power of the Chinese threat. Our adversaries wrote up their long-term plans in 1999 and have been executing them relentlessly ever since. Our leaders have a moral obligation to understand what's happening, sound the alarm, wake up the country, and inspire Americans of all political stripes to do everything in their power to stop this totalitarian regime.

I also want the average American to have access to this book. It's time for every influential person in America—policy makers, diplomats, business executives, investors, journalists, scientists, academics, and more—to become part of the resistance to the Chinese Communist Party.

My hope is that by explaining *Unrestricted Warfare* and its consequences, this book will make it impossible for my fellow Americans to continue to deny the reality of our existential conflict with China. The simple, chilling truth is that the CCP is doing everything in its power, mostly via economics, technology, diplomacy, and the media—not yet via military power—to destroy our way of life. To understand that plan, you need to understand *Unrestricted Warfare*. The stakes couldn't be higher.

Rob Spalding
Brigadier General USAF (ret.)
October 15, 2021

WAR WITHOUT RULES

CHAPTER 1

KNOW YOUR ENEMY

"TO KNOW YOUR ENEMY, YOU MUST BECOME YOUR ENEMY." That is from Sun Tzu, the font of much Chinese strategic wisdom. He means: See the situation through your enemy's eyes. How would he react if the circumstances were reversed? What steps would he take to gain advantage? Where are his weak points? When it came to the outbreak of SARS-CoV-2, not only did we not see the problem through the eyes of China's Communist leaders, we didn't even realize they were the enemy.

In January 2020, Americans believed what the Chinese told them—that the virus was under control. Why would they lie about something as serious as a deadly disease? But even as we believed them, the Chinese Communist Party was locking down its own country while allowing international flights out of Wuhan, knowing that Wuhan residents would carry the virus to the rest of the world, perhaps escalating it into a global pandemic. It made the cold-blooded calculation that COVID-19 could actually help China if it weakened the United States and Europe.

The CCP also began a global disinformation campaign, led by their hordes of "50 Cent Army" members. This wasn't a conventional army—it was a group of social media agents who got paid 50 cents in Chinese renminbi for every post they'd make on Western social media platforms. The disinformation campaign shared positive stories about the CCP's response to COVID-19, making it seem far more effective than it actually was, while downplaying the severity and contagiousness of the virus. At the same time, Chinese officials refused to tell the World Health Organization about the outbreak for many weeks, in violation of their agreement. Meanwhile, all those international travelers who flew out of Wuhan and other Chinese cities were carrying the virus across Asia, into Europe, and soon after to the United States. And how is it conceivable that China muzzled its doctors and refused to share the genetic sequence and virus samples or allow outside scientists into China to study the origins and formulate treatment—to this day?

Thanks to COVID-19, by late 2020, the world's major economies would lose an estimated $4 trillion in economic output—and eventually more than five million people would die. In addition to reopening their economy faster than the West, the Chinese owned the means to mass produce many of the goods the West urgently needed, like ventilators and personal protective equipment. They would also gain a propaganda victory as they found yet another reason to point to U.S. failings while falsely praising their own conduct by rewriting and burying history.

For the Chinese leadership, COVID was not a problem, it was an opportunity. It was a weapon to be used to advance the interests of China. Whether or not it was a deliberate or accidental release from the Wuhan lab—we may never know—everything that followed was an orchestrated response that caused havoc for the rest of the world.

If these consequences of the CCP's actions had been the result of a conventional military attack, America would have surely retaliated. But instead, this kind of stealth war—combining ruthless economic policies, indifference to the public good, and a weaponization of the internet—attracted minimal attention. While conspiracy theorists speculated that the Chinese had designed COVID-19 in a lab as a bioweapon, few Americans discussed the less extreme but proven case: that the CCP took advantage of a surprise crisis to advance its own interests and hurt its adversaries. They had started lying to the public from the moment of local physician Dr. Li Wenliang's warning, and they're still lying about Chinese COVID statistics as I write this in late 2021.

Looking back, we can see that the United States ignored that hoary military maxim of know your enemy. How different would the early days of the COVID epidemic have been if we had taken a much harsher view of the Chinese Communist Party and had not been distracted by the false and foolish notion that any criticism of the Chinese government was racist. But we did not understand what our enemy wanted and we did not understand their game.

What China Wants

Knowing the goals and motives of any country is at the foundation of diplomacy and national security—most keenly when you're talking about a budding superpower with a giant army and nuclear weapons. Fundamentally, you want to know if your adversaries are a threat, and if so, what kind of threat? Are they willing and able to go to war with their neighbors? Do they want territory? Resources? Control over global trade? Is there a scenario in which they would invade the United States? National security analysts, as I once was, look for clues in speeches by party bosses, bread crumbs in academic papers, phrases of military doctrine. Always, we're standing outside a murky window peering in. Or trying to find a clear window. I think *Unrestricted Warfare* is that window. Once we establish *what* the Chinese are up to, *UW* will help us understand the *how* and *why*.

Winston Churchill famously said of Soviet Russia, "It is a riddle wrapped in a mystery inside an enigma." He was trying to see into the mind of Joseph Stalin and his Communist Party henchmen in the Kremlin. American leaders at the height of the Cold War asked a thousand times, "What is Russia up to? What do they want? How dangerous are they?" We eventually figured them out. Thanks to some keen analysis and the fortitude of President Ronald Reagan, we divined that Russia was a hollow country with a fragile economy and a bloated military—a jackbooted clown show plagued by an endless series of economic disasters that ultimately proved communism, and the Communist party, a failure. Reagan's arms race drove them over the cliff.

It would be a mistake, however, to put China in the same box. Beijing's motives are much more obscure than Moscow's, and the biggest error our leaders can make today is thinking they have a clear understanding of what the CCP wants and how it is getting it.

It's easy to think we have some understanding of our rival. We have, after all, fought bloody battles against the Chinese army during the Korean War. The Chinese have fought shooting wars with India and Vietnam over disputed territory. More recently, because there wasn't much fear of military action, there has been a general assumption in our diplomatic and military community that China is not a direct threat to the United States. Or, if they are, that we can control them by putting pressure on them in all of the normal ways.

But we can't rerun the Soviet movie and expect the same outcome. China is a bigger problem. Yes, they made the same colossal economic blunders under Mao—resulting in millions of deaths from starvation. Their ghastly political purges drained its society of its talent before the 1980s. But they survived. Thrived, even. And since then have arguably made few mistakes. Remember that their economy dwarfs Russia's, as does their population of 1.4 billion people. Their version of communism is much more complex than the Soviet's, allowing free enterprise with a leash. And the Chinese culture has taken to entrepreneurship in a way that Russia's has not. China's military is now formidable. Whether from research and development or theft, they are a technologically advanced nation. Their money has given them far more global entrée than the Soviet's blunt force ever could. They have their problems, which I'll discuss later. But the big lesson is: China is not Russia 2.0.

So what is China up to? What do they want? And how are they working to get it?

According to too many of our politicians and business leaders, China doesn't want much, and it isn't acting against us at all. Conversations on this subject that take place in the Pentagon are usually steered by the view from the top. In some fashion, the views of the president and his most senior advisers and cabinet members set the tone for how the meetings would go. In my tours in both the White House national security staff and the Pentagon, the required view was that if you said China was an enemy, you could be out of a job. Outside the formality of those rooms, my colleagues and I had screaming arguments about exactly that subject.

When I arrived at the Pentagon as the China adviser to the chairman of the Joint Chiefs of Staff in 2014, the instructions from the Obama administration were clear: We were not going to do anything in public to antagonize China as their relationship is too significant financially. The narrative was that the two most powerful countries in the world had to cooperate to solve greater challenges like a nuclear-armed North Korea and climate change. That stance was built on the absurd idea that China wants to fix either of these issues. (It doesn't.)

Over those years I came to two key realizations. First, the number one goal of the Chinese Communist Party is the survival of the Chinese Communist Party. And second, the number one threat to achieving that goal is American democracy. We may not see them as our enemy, but they surely see us as their enemy. An existential one.

The basis of globalization that was agreed to in the wake of World War II was the principles of the Atlantic Charter, which underlies the United Nations, the World Trade Organization, and other bodies. There are four keys: free markets, democratic principles, rule of law, and self-determination. This is what the global elites who convene in places like Davos believed the Chinese were moving toward. In fact, the exact opposite was true. As we later learned, the Chinese Communist Party regards those exact principles as a fundamental threat to its existence.

The People's Republic of China has a constitution, but it is superseded by the Communist Party constitution, which makes clear that the sovereign power of China—the ruler—is the party. And the ruler of the party—in theory the Central Committee, but in reality President Xi Jinping—is the ruler of the country. His cadres are the 90 million party members, a privileged class among their 1,350,000,000 other fellow citizens. No surprise, there are many good reasons to keep the party in charge. And to suppress Western ideas.

This was made most clear to me in one of those rare glimpses of internal thinking. Document No. 9 was a party directive to those many local officials that leaked in 2013. At the time, Xi was new to the job and there was great hope in Washington that the tidy, well-dressed gentleman was going to launch the next phase of reform. To those who knew how to read it, Document No. 9 smothered that hope. Issued from the Central Committee, it attacked a growing reform movement and told the local leaders in no uncertain terms that China was a staunchly Communist country and that Western ideals were to be crushed. Forbidden were notions of constitutional democracy, a free press, examinations into China's troubled history, economic privatization. The reform advocates were subversives whose "goal is to obscure the essential differences between the West's value system and the value system we advocate, ultimately using the West's value systems to supplant the core values of Socialism."

These ideas were threats to be guarded against. And soon after began a series of arrests and detentions of human rights lawyers, academics, and journalists.

In Washington, there was not much concern. The complexity of China's actions across so many fronts had made it a "Not my job" issue for so many U.S. agencies. What did the Pentagon care about the arrest of journalists in Shenzhen or the infringement of some Silicon Valley company's patent? What did the Commerce Department care about man-made military islands in the South China Sea? No one was seeing the whole picture.

While America's leaders had become complacent—reasoning that communism was dead and America ascendant—leaders of the CCP were strategizing how to become the new global superpower by 2049, the one hundredth anniversary of the Communist takeover of China. As far back as the Tiananmen Square protests of 1989, the CCP saw how essential it was to block out the Western concepts of free speech and democracy, even while importing Western capital and technology. Indoctrination and thought control became more important than ever. That's why all the Chinese actions fit together in a mosaic that would have made Mao proud.

China's Strategy

It's not enough to know what your enemy wants. You need to understand his strategy. This is where Americans are really confused. We are primed to fight in one way—all-out war—and see aggression through the same lens. The Chinese are doing something else.

It was some briefings I received from friends in the U.S. corporate community that finally made clear to me the extent of the Chinese invasion. Some smart people with money at stake indeed saw the whole picture. The Chinese were already fighting an "everywhere war," and the question to ask was, Where was it going next?

They explained how the CCP has been acquiring technology without paying a cent toward developing it, carefully taking control of the world's shipping businesses, infiltrating our corporations and scientific laboratories, using American investor dollars to finance its factories and companies—and then insisting that any profits stay in China. This is just one example of how China is surreptitiously fighting for world domination—regional and global hegemony in the words of the academics.

Consider some of their other methods:

China has been fighting us in the "free market." Our political and business elites have failed to realize that the CCP has not played by the rules of international law and the assumptions of the many global organizations into which they have recently been welcomed. They have failed to recognize that the Chinese state and private sector work together to steal intellectual property—theft is not an accident; it's part of the business model.

They failed to realize that a Westernized China would use its increasingly sophisticated surveillance technology to create a new Orwellian system of "social credit scores" that reward or punish citizens depending on evidence of their dedication to the Communist Party. Our elites assume the military is the main weapon in a war, failing to realize that money is stronger. They've not realized that Chinese money was used to sway political leaders in foreign countries, silence ideas, and purchase or steal technology. It was being used to manufacture goods at dirt-cheap prices and drive competitors out of business. It created an army of academics who fanned out to gather or steal scientific, technological, or engineering intelligence.

By infiltrating the web of social media, China has acquired the ability to manipulate and distort all manner of information. Consider these headlines: "China Forces Disney to Make China-Friendly Movies"; "A National Basketball Association Team Almost Fires a Top Executive After He Makes Some Mild Criticism of Forced-Labor Camps in Western China"; "*The New York Times* Discovers That the CCP Propaganda Machine Has Seeded Social Media with Thousands of Bogus, Mass-Manufactured Videos from Supposed Uyghur Minorities Who Proclaimed How Well Treated They Were." We are led to think that all the volumes of documentation of the abuse and even genocide of the Muslim Uyghurs was a Western lie!

The Uyghur operation was typical of a vast and expanding attempt to reshape public opinion in China's favor for both a domestic and an international audience. *The Washington Post* editorial page saw the significance of the Chinese turning our own love of freedom against us: "The recently unearthed operation reveals China's continued intention to exploit the openness of the United States, its allies and the technology companies their citizens rely on to spread false and regime-friendly political narratives—even as the Great Firewall shuts the rest of the world out for fear that true and critical narratives could make their way in."

China is also complicit in the American drug epidemic. In 2019, after years of pleading from the United States, China said it would crack down on the production of fentanyl, a lab-produced opioid fifty times more powerful than heroin. That year, thirty-seven thousand people died in the United States from fentanyl overdoses. The year after the "crackdown" there were fifty-seven thousand overdose deaths. As the Brookings Institution summarized in a July 2020 report, "Since 2013, China has been the principal source of the fentanyl flooding the U.S. illicit drug market—or the precursor agents from which fentanyl is produced, often in Mexico—fueling the deadliest drug epidemic in U.S. history." Brookings went on to explain a pattern of Chinese behavior over the years, in which they first deny the problem, then say they will act, but can't seem to muster the law enforcement resources necessary. And the United States pushes them to try harder. Really? Knowing the principles of *Unrestricted Warfare* and the comprehensive police powers of the Chinese surveillance state, do we believe that they can't shut down an industry that just happens to export one more destructive product causing havoc in the United States?

On climate change, gullible environmentalists and government officials have been conned by another set of China's lies. Indeed, the Biden administration—like that of President Obama—still believes that working with China on climate is so important and achievable that it should excuse bad behavior in other areas. *National Review* quoted an assessment of China's internal plans by the Institute for Energy Research: "With its March [2021] release of a new five-year plan (FYP), the 14th in its history, China has embarrassed its climate cheerleaders in the West. Beijing's plan institutes no carbon cap, no coal phase-out, and no roadmap by which it will execute upon Xi's words. Despite the carbon-neutral-by-2060 pledge, the

FYP emphasizes the importance of coal to China's continued development, not the emissions that come with its use."

All of the tactics outlined here have more to do with thuggery than diplomacy. But the ends—increasing the CCP's influence over not just foreign governments and corporations but also over media outlets, religious groups, academics, civil rights groups, and, at a frighteningly granular level, individual citizens—justify the means. China routinely ignores international trade laws, property laws, environmental laws, drug laws, and pretty much any other law that stands in its way.

Far from being the worst of China's misdeeds, Chinese complicity in the spread of COVID-19 is just a wake-up call. China is fighting us on every front, in ways visible and invisible.

Seeing Their Strategy

The stakes for understanding China's war are high. We've already seen the consequences of its stealth invasion of Hong Kong, with totalitarian restrictions clamping down on a once-free society. China's vaunted Belt and Road Initiative is making vassals of two thirds of the world. China now has significant nuclear missiles that bring its arsenal on par with that of the United States and Russia. Xi Jinping's hostile rhetoric is growing bolder: "The Chinese people will never allow foreign forces to bully, oppress or enslave us," he said on the one hundredth anniversary of the party's founding, adding that "whoever nurses delusions of doing so will crack their heads and spill blood on the Great Wall of steel built from the flesh and blood of 1.4 billion Chinese people."

No one should doubt that China is playing for keeps and, at the moment, believes it is winning.

I spent a lot of my career arguing with other analysts over the question of what China wants. We now have the answer. As Xi Jinping has made clear, the goal of the CCP is the full ascendance of China as the sole world power by 2049—one hundred years after the Communist takeover of China. The path to that goal is by whatever means necessary. The obstacle on that path is the United States.

Thanks in part to COVID-19, the United States and other nations have begun to make a louder response to Chinese actions, at least verbally. But so far it is not nearly enough, especially when you understand the pattern of their behavior.

If we are to have any chance of China going the same way as the USSR, we need to face our ignorance. We need to accept that China is a different kind of enemy from the USSR. We need to accept that they want to destroy us. We need to accept that China is fighting against us in ways we don't even realize. And we need to find a window into the CCP's war room.

Fortunately, we do have one clear window: *Unrestricted Warfare,* the Chinese war manual that lays out their goals and their strategies. It puts in a modern context some of the enduring principles set down centuries ago in the military classic *The Art of War* and adapted over the years. Among them:

Know the Face of War. It has changed over time. Combined, unrestricted war seeks victory through nonviolent means, but does not rule out violence.

Know Your Enemy. Study his strengths and weaknesses and match them to your own.

Create One-Minded Forces. Every aspect of military and civilian action should be coordinated.

Bring the People into Harmony with Their Leaders. Focus all of society on achieving your objective.

The book explains how and why China fights war without rules, and if you had read it, none of what we've seen recently would surprise you. If our leaders read it, they can understand new ways of thwarting the Chinese invasion.

Let's start to study the book.

CHAPTER 2

A NEW WAY OF WAR

UNRESTRICTED WARFARE WAS WRITTEN MORE THAN TWENTY years ago by two colonels in the People's Liberation Army but has taken its place alongside such military classics as Sun Tzu's *The Art of War.*

In the late 1990s, the end of the U.S.-Soviet Cold War leaves the United States as the sole global superpower. While the Chinese Communist Party has been following, since the days of Mao, its march to long-dreamed-of dominance, the road looks very long. The Chinese leadership is asking themselves important questions about where they go next. Col. Qiao Liang and Col. Wang Xiangsui, part of a strategic think tank within the People's Liberation Army, believe they have a good idea. Their words will find their way into the hands of the Communist Party leadership that shapes the direction of the country, as well as the tightly controlled handful of military and political academies that train the thousands of cadres who execute those orders. Following the Persian Gulf War of 1990, the Chinese colonels were tasked with studying America's strategies during that conflict. The war itself was short, brutal, and successful. So much so that for America it's become a historical footnote—overshadowed by the disastrous aftermath of Gulf War Two in 2003. But the colonels saw that something significant had happened.

Before the Gulf War, the world had never seen a victory so rapid and so total.

Think of Gen. Colin L. Powell, the chairman of the Joint Chiefs of Staff, standing calmly in front of the international press corps and explaining how we would fight Operation Desert Storm. "Our strategy to go after this army is very, very simple. First, we're going to cut it off, and then we're going to kill it."

He made good on that promise within about a month. There were tank battles the Americans won 50–0. The Iraqi air force was, as Powell promised, ripped apart while still on the ground. If any planes got into the air, they were shot dead from so far away they never saw it coming. The bombing of crucial sites was precise and deadly. The Navy controlled the Gulf itself and launched strikes from an invincible cocoon.

Some of the most devastating weapons were unseen. Hellfire missiles and laser-guided bombs destroyed air defense systems and disabled communications. The Iraqi army was quickly a blind, bleeding palooka staggering back to its corner. That's when the last devastating blow came. The "Highway of Death" was where the retreating elements of the Iraqi army were turned into a molten metal graveyard by precision bombing.

But it was the success of nonlethal weapons that caught the

attention of some top leaders. The United States can win without resorting to weapons of mass destruction. Destroying communications and power facilities preserved lives but crippled the enemy. "Attrition warfare belongs to another age, and the days when wars could be won by sheer bravery and perseverance are gone," wrote John Warden, a U.S. Air Force colonel, known as the architect of the Gulf War. "Victory will go to those who think through the problem and capitalize on every tool available."

The American victory was indeed a masterpiece of technology, tactics, and execution. If you were a pro, as the colonels were, you had to sit back in admiration. And then you had to think: What does this mean for China?

The leaders of the Chinese Communist Party looked at the world in the late 1990s and saw an existential threat to their hundred-year march toward global domination. They had to avoid spending themselves into bankruptcy via military buildup, as the Soviet Union had done. They also had to prevent their citizens from rising in protest and revolution, as the East Germans and other Communist bloc peoples had done. China in the early 1990s was still essentially a developing country with a largely rural economy and hundreds of millions of poor citizens. The remarkable rise of industrialization was underway, but China's economy had far to go.

At that time, the Chinese army was larger but likely not better than the now-devastated Iraqi forces. If America could essentially destroy the Iraqi military so quickly and cheaply using Warden's high-tech tactics, what could it do to China during a nonnuclear engagement?

The colonels concluded that above all they had to avoid provoking the awesome military might of the United States and its Western allies, as Saddam Hussein had foolishly done. The risks of direct military engagement with the West had escalated beyond the point that it could ever be acceptable.

In short, the CCP needed a new plan for the next phase of China's march toward preeminence by 2049. They needed to keep a low profile while waging a stealth war on the West that didn't seem like a war at all. A new, unprecedented kind of war that the Americans, NATO, the World Trade Organization, and the United Nations wouldn't understand, let alone know how to oppose. China would have to avoid the spotlight while other global actors—such as the Taliban, Al Qaeda, Iran, Russia, and North Korea—could distract the West as the world's bad guys.

Qiao and Wang wrote exactly the plan the CCP needed. It is a doctrine that says essentially "everything is war." They said that modern wars could be fought beyond traditional military means, or with no military at all. Civilians needed to be warriors too, and battlefields could be about information, economies, technology, the environment, and more. Finally, that this kind of war—unrestricted war, war without rules—needed to be permanent. They published their thesis on January 17, 1999, the eighth anniversary of the start of the Persian Gulf War. It has lived a long life since then.

The colonels didn't invent the notion of unrestricted war, but they did a good job of consolidating it into a doctrine that was read, and acted upon, by military and political leaders. They pulled together centuries of Chinese thinking about warfare and made it relevant in a modern context. They laid out a coherent vision of how to achieve power at a time when Chinese leaders had grand ambitions but little real power. *Unrestricted Warfare* codified ongoing efforts and justified new theories, such as using the emerging technology sector, to disrupt the world order. It put on paper ideas that were already ingrained in the minds of many of the Communist Party elite, who were nonetheless frustrated at their inability to move more aggressively against the main enemy, the United States. Read in the military academies and party think tanks, it was the right book at the right time.

"The first rule of unrestricted warfare," said Col. Qiao Liang, "is that there are no rules, with nothing forbidden."

Though Qiao and Wang were military officers, they aspired to be much more than military strategists. They also saw themselves as serious thinkers about economics, politics, diplomacy, and the ever-growing power of technology to exploit and control humanity.

What they created was not so much a strategy but a form of doctrine. It is a series of principles that they hoped would guide decision-making and help others shape specific strategies. But unlike a classic doctrine that might emerge from the Pentagon with terse language and a tightly organized structure, the colonels indulge their love of philosophy and history, meandering at times to discuss Mongol cavalry tactics, the use of tanks in World War I, and centuries of Chinese thinking.

They elaborate a "new warfare," which is much like China's

age-old notion of winning without necessarily using violence. Instead, they propose "political, economic and technological violence."

The point is: "Using all means, including armed force or non-armed force, military and non-military, and lethal and non-lethal means to compel the enemy to accept one's interest." Or, in a more ominous summary: "To force the enemy to serve one's own interests."

Specifics fill the book: Psychological warfare involving false rumors to create dissension. Media warfare to undermine the political systems of rivals. Large-scale espionage to steal business secrets. Smuggling warfare to manipulate markets. Drug warfare to spread social chaos. Disrupting financial markets. Dominating international organizations, such as those managing trade relations or global health issues, to one's advantage. Attacking key infrastructure such as electricity or phone networks. And, of course, biowarfare.

There is a profound amorality to their vision. To be ignored are the rules and limits forged by liberal-minded nations over centuries: things like the Geneva Conventions or the hundreds of international organizations that try to regulate fair trade, global health, sustainable fishing, and an infinite number of other common necessities.

They were particularly prescient about the military power of technology, computers, and the nascent internet. They saw the "computer hacker" as the first line of attack and predicted "organized hacker warfare launched by a state," which was exposed in July 2021 by the entire Western alliance.

"In a world where even 'nuclear warfare' will perhaps become obsolete military jargon," they write in their sometimes florid prose, "it is likely that the pasty-faced scholar wearing thick eyeglasses is better suited to be a modern soldier than is a young lowbrow with bulging biceps.... The digital fighter is taking over the role formerly played by the 'blood and iron' warrior."

These multiple options should be used often and in combination, a concept they call "addition." They talk at length about the amplifying effect of doing many things in combination—or "beyond-limits combined war." It makes, they write, "a cocktail mixture of warfare."

Which leads to a conclusion at once goofy and chilling: "It can be affirmed that whoever is able to mix a tasty and unique cocktail for the future banquet of war will ultimately be able to wear the laurels of success on his own head."

Their work inspired other books that added more specifics to the doctrine, strategy, and tactics. It is why the People's Liberation Army—the combat army, not the intelligence services—is the main employer of hundreds of thousands of hackers, censors, propaganda specialists, and biowarfare experts, among others. But none of those works provides the detailed, comprehensive vision that, if we look closely enough, we are now able to see enacted on a daily basis by the Chinese leadership.

The Chinese Way of War

To truly understand their work, we need to start with the many ideas—some thousands of years old, others shaped by recent events when they were working on *UW*—that influenced Qiao and Wang. There are fundamental differences between Western and Eastern cultures, not the least as they relate to international relations and warfare. Since the Peace of Westphalia, when European sovereigns made a fragile bargain to stop their own centuries of unrestricted and endless war, Western nations have viewed international disputes as discrete problems to be solved through diplomacy or, when diplomacy fails, through war. As the German military theorist Carl von Clausewitz famously put it two centuries ago, "War is the continuation of politics by other means." This attitude was the foundation of America's rise to superpower status and its guiding principle during the Cold War.

But the cultures of the Far East, especially China, have always seen international relations holistically, focusing on the big picture rather than narrow objectives. Leading Chinese military strategists, from Sun Tzu through Mao Zedong, focused on the art of patiently outmaneuvering an adversary over the long term, ideally without using violence. In many ways, it is the opposite of Clausewitz: *Politics is the continuation of war by other means.* And because politics is permanent, so is war.

The authors of *Unrestricted Warfare* were students of history who understood the differences. In fact, there has often been tension between military experts who focused on refining the art and science of using military power and politicians who restrained the use of military force for the sake of diplomacy or other priorities. This tension within the Western powers became an opportunity for the Chinese to exploit after the rise of the CCP in the mid-twentieth century.

Western leaders tended to look for one of the traditional tools in their toolbox, such as negotiation, confrontation, sanctions, or, if necessary, war. All of those fields had separate experts—from diplomats to trade policy experts to military strategists—who naturally saw the most value in their respective fields. Meanwhile, the Chinese saw all those approaches to conflict as part of a single overarching approach—a competition for supremacy by any means necessary.

Writing in 1998, the colonels declare an end to the old Western rules: "The modern concept of 'nation states' which emerged from the Peace of Westphalia in 1648 is no longer the sole representative occupying the top position in social, political, economic and cultural organizations. . . . the inherent contradictions between one nation and another, are presenting an unprecedented challenge to national authority, national interests and national will."

Clausewitz, in his influential 1832 treatise *On War,* laid out some other basic Western assumptions: Whenever disputes arose, various attempts should first be made to resolve those disputes peacefully, with war following only as a necessary last resort. Western war theory held that war should be limited. Clausewitz's great rival as a nineteenth-century military theorist was the French general Antoine-Henri de Jomini, who in 1838 published *Précis de l'art de la guerre* (*Summary of the Art of War*). Jomini argued that the amount of force deployed should be kept to the minimum necessary in order to reduce casualties. Rather than using force indiscriminately or attempting to cause the most damage possible, leaders should concentrate their combat power at the decisive point that would most quickly cause the enemy to surrender. Jomini's goal was to make warfare secondary to the political goals of the state. As he wrote:

"We will suppose an army taking the field: the first care of its commander should be to agree with the head of the state upon the character of the war: then he must carefully study the theater of war, and select the most suitable base of operations, taking into consideration the frontiers of the state and those of its allies."

The Chinese colonels diverge from these Western theorists pretty clearly. Unlike Clausewitz, they argue that *even before* a nation crosses the line into violent warfare, there is no need to adhere to self-imposed restrictions. Like Jomini, they make a case for restraint, but a specific kind intended to protect a country from overcommitting and leaving itself vulnerable to counterattack.

It's no great surprise that the colonels would have a different view on war. For thousands of years, Chinese culture has defined war more holistically than the West, focusing on long-term, often vague objectives that many times had to do with the restoration of Chinese greatness rather than clearly defined short-term victories. The most important thing is overcoming your adversary, and it doesn't really matter whether your primary method is military, diplomatic, or economic.

This kind of thinking goes all the way back to Sun Tzu, the Chinese military strategist, general, and philosopher who lived about twenty-five hundred years ago (or possibly was one of several strategists contributing to the classic treatise). It's hard to overstate the enduring influence of *The Art of War* across all those centuries of Chinese dynasties rising and falling. For instance, during the pivotal Warring States period, 475 to 221 B.C., various leaders and their armies engaged in shifting alliances, secret missions, and betrayals that could have fit into the fictional world of *Game of Thrones.* They all studied and tried to apply *The Art of War,* as did future generations of warriors, politicians, and businesspeople.

You can find Sun Tzu quoted all over the internet on many aspects of strategy. But to me, his most significant theme is that warfare is merely one part of the bigger effort to advance national interests and dominate one's enemies. Consider these quotes, which seem almost pacifist for a book that many people assume (before they actually read it) must be all about the use of force:

- "Appear weak when you are strong, and strong when you are weak."
- "The supreme art of war is to subdue the enemy without fighting."
- "Victorious warriors win first and then go to war, while defeated warriors go to war first and then seek to win."
- "There is no instance of a nation benefitting from prolonged warfare."
- "All warfare is based on deception. Hence, when we are able to attack, we must seem unable; when using our forces, we must appear inactive; when we are near, we must make the enemy believe we are far away; when far away, we must make him believe we are near."
- "Move not unless you see an advantage; use not your troops unless there is something to be gained; fight not unless the position is critical."
- "The wise warrior avoids the battle."

One reason Sun Tzu's philosophy made such an impact was that China was always large and hard to defend from outside invaders, especially the Mongols to the north. Fear of invasion led to the extensive fortification of the Great Wall during the Ming Dynasty of 1368–1644. But underneath their shared focus on keeping out the Mongols, rival Chinese leaders focused on political infighting, intrigue, and shifting alliances. These challenges gave them added incentives to avoid war unless absolutely necessary, as well as incentives to forge alliances and, if necessary, buy off their rivals. This tradition helped establish the way that the Chinese think about warfare, right up to the present.

United States Air Force fighter pilot turned military strategist John Boyd addressed the ongoing influence of Sun Tzu in a famous briefing presentation, Patterns of Conflict, which he delivered at the Pentagon in 1986. He noted that Western commanders traditionally focused on winning battles while Chinese commanders sought ways to disrupt the adversary prior to battle—ideally making the battle unnecessary. They tried to avoid protracted war by applying Sun Tzu's ancient but still effective strategies:

- Probe the enemy's organization and dispositions to unmask his strengths, weaknesses, patterns of movement, and intentions.
- Shape the enemy's perceptions of the world to manipulate his plans and actions.
- Disrupt the enemy's alliances before directly attacking his army.

• If fighting is necessary, focus strength quickly and unexpectedly against his weaknesses.*

François Jullien, a French philosopher and sinologist, has also
studied the Chinese tradition of winning without fighting. His
2004 book, *A Treatise on Efficacy: Between Western and Chinese
Thinking*, noted that Western strategists like Clausewitz couldn't
conceive of warfare without a "plan of war" devised in advance.
That plan became "the framework for the whole act of war," which
could put Western military forces at a disadvantage whenever
reality deviated sharply from the projected outcome. As Jullien
wrote:

> The ancient Chinese tell us that it is enough to know how
> to make the most of the way a situation develops and to let
> yourself be "carried" along by it. . . . Chinese thought regards
> the whole of reality as a regulated and continuous process
> that stems purely from the interaction of the factors in play
> (which are at once opposed and complementary: the famous
> yin and yang). Order is not perceived as coming from a model
> that one can fix one's eyes on and apply to things. . . .
>
> The Chinese sage never conceived of a contemplative ac-
> tivity that was pure knowledge, possessing an end in itself,
> or that itself represented the supreme end (happiness) and

---

*John Boyd, "Patterns of Conflict," Air Power Australia, http://www.ausairpower.net/JRB
/poc.pdf.

was altogether disinterested. For him, the "world" was not an object of speculation; it was not a matter of "knowledge" on the one hand and "action" on the other. That is why Chinese thought, logically enough, disregarded the theory-practice relationship: not through ignorance or because it was childish, but simply because it sidestepped the concept.*

The Communist Way of War

There is history even earlier than Sun Tzu that may help us understand the philosophy of war without rules. In 638 B.C., the Song Kingdom and Chu Kingdom fought for control of the Central Plains. Their armies faced each other on the banks of the Hong River. The Chu army was the stronger but had to cross the river to engage its enemies. Some of the Song officials proposed surprising their opponents by attacking as the first elements came ashore and the rest were crossing. This went against the military conventions of the time, which called for armies to complete their formations before the attack began. The Song ruler, Duke Xiang, overruled his advisers, waited patiently for his enemy, lost the battle, and was badly wounded. His failure became an object lesson through history, with the philosopher Han Feizi calling it "the scourge of pro-righteousness." Mao Zedong once commented that the Duke's Battle of Hong River showed "a stupid pig-like benevolence and morality." This perhaps is the origin of unrestricted warfare.

---

*François Jullien, *A Treatise on Efficacy*, trans. Janet Lloyd (Honolulu: University of Hawai'i Press, 2004), vii–viii, 15, https://uberty.org/wp-content/uploads/2015/10/francois-jullien-treatise-on-efficacy-between-western-and-chinese-thinking.pdf.

The colonels also draw on more recent Chinese war theory. When Mao Zedong rose to power in 1949 as the leader of the Communist revolution, he inherited five thousand years of Chinese tradition. He was an avid reader of ancient philosophy and history and applied them to his conception of a "people's war" that would, over the long term, make China the dominant superpower on Earth. Mao was willing to wait patiently for the chance to avenge all the humiliations that the West had imposed on China since the mid-nineteenth century, including the British navy's destruction of its ports during the Opium Wars, the European pressures that led to the collapse of the Qing Dynasty in 1912, Japan's seizures of Korea and Manchuria, and the West's support of Chiang Kai-shek during the twentieth-century Chinese Civil War.

In fact, Mao framed his methodical, long-term plan as a "hundred-year marathon" to defeat the West. And he resolved that over that coming century, the CCP would make every effort to avoid direct military confrontation with the United States, Europe, or other powers. This overarching strategy allowed Mao to focus on inward-facing initiatives, including China's Great Leap Forward in 1958 to industrialize its economy and attempts at agrarian reforms, which backfired horribly and killed tens of millions during the Great Famine of 1959–61. The hundred-year marathon also underpinned the brutal Cultural Revolution of 1966–76, which terrorized, "reeducated," and killed millions of civilians to lock in the CCP's total control over every aspect of the Chinese economy, culture, and private life.

During all those upheavals in the 1950s and 1960s, Mao tried to avoid direct military conflict with the West. He depicted China as the junior partner of the Soviet Union in their Communist alliance, reinforcing the West's perception of China as relatively harmless and backward, and a much lesser threat than the USSR. Mao was happy to let Stalin and his successors support potential Communist revolutions in Africa, Latin America, and elsewhere while China pretended to be poor and weak.

Although nearly three million Chinese troops and civilians supported the North Korean army during the Korean War of 1950–53, Mao concluded that, with nearly a million dead and wounded, this proxy war was a terrible use of resources in the context of the hundred-year marathon. Likewise, China's military support of North Vietnam during the Vietnam War was seen as an unfortunate distraction, wasting billions of dollars.

By 1967, China's nuclear program had created its first hydrogen bomb, but Mao never sought a massive nuclear arsenal comparable to that of the Soviet Union's. His goal was to build just enough nuclear missiles to deter the United States from interfering in Taiwan or North Korea, but not enough to drain China of essential resources. He was happy to let the USSR spend itself into bankruptcy while drawing global criticism as the malevolent instigator of nuclear proliferation. Meanwhile, China could quietly focus on building its economy and its nonnuclear military capacity.

Mao's outreach to the Nixon administration in the early 1970s, including an invitation to President Richard Nixon and Secretary of State Henry Kissinger to visit Beijing as honored guests, was his next strategic masterstroke. Sun Tzu would have been proud of how Mao used Nixon's hunger for a foreign policy triumph against him. By deferring to the United States, the CCP won access to American investment and technology while reinforcing China's image as an underdeveloped nation that was far less threatening than the USSR. The Nixon administration bragged about "opening" China, without even realizing how this would help China far more than the United States in the long term. It was a classic example of dominating an enemy without combat—of deploying diplomacy and trade as warfare by other means.

For the next fifteen years, the United States would support China as part of our Cold War strategy of destabilizing the Soviet Union. American companies began to do more and more business in China, embracing the very American mindset that politics, business, and military conflict had little or nothing to do with one another. And American politicians would mostly look the other way at China's totalitarian, antidemocratic system and its horrifying record of human rights abuses. Most Americans were convinced that introducing capitalism and free trade would inevitably make China more liberal, leading to future reforms that would improve the lives of ordinary Chinese citizens.

Unfortunately, this consensus among American politicians, policy experts, business leaders, and investors was nothing more than magical thinking. It endured through Mao's death in 1976 and the rise of Deng Xiaoping as "paramount leader" of the CCP and the Chinese government in 1978. Magical thinking continued through the booming economy of the 1980s as China benefited from more and more foreign investment and global trade. In the meantime, instead of inching toward democracy, the CCP maintained an iron grip on all facets of Chinese life, including a total rejection of human rights, civil liberties, or the rule of law.

Then came the Tiananmen Square crisis of 1989 and the critical decade that paved the way for *Unrestricted Warfare.*

The Legacy of Tiananmen Square

For three weeks starting in May 1989, ordinary Chinese citizens—students, workers, civil rights leaders—gathered in Beijing's historic Tiananmen Square for rallies in support of democracy and civil rights. The protests had been set off in April after the death of the pro-reform Communist general secretary Hu Yaobang. Many Chinese were feeling anxious after a decade of economic reforms that had moved China toward a market economy but seemed to be benefiting only CCP insiders instead of the general population. Additional grievances included inflation, corruption, and restrictions on political participation.

The ranks of the protesters in the square grew steadily, peaking at about a million by late May. The CCP had never seen anything remotely like these protests in the forty years since the Communist Revolution. The daily drama in the square drew media attention around the world, especially when the protesters erected a thirty-three-foot-high statue out of foam and papier-mâché, which they modeled after the Statue of Liberty. They called it the Goddess of Democracy. Observers around the world wondered if this was China's equivalent of 1776 in the United States or 1789 in France.

But by June 2, Deng Xiaoping and his inner circle were plotting to clear Tiananmen Square and restore their control over Beijing, by force if necessary. Martial law was imposed on June 3, with protesters warned to stay inside, but many remained in the square to confront the approaching army. The Goddess of Democracy was destroyed on June 4, when the army moved violently against the protesters. On June 5, the suppression of the protests was immortalized around the world via video footage and photographs of a lone man standing defiantly in front of a column of tanks in Tiananmen Square—the anonymous, iconic "Tank Man," whose identity and fate remain a mystery to this day.

The number of Chinese civilians killed by the army in Tiananmen Square has never been confirmed, with estimates ranging from a few hundred to about ten thousand. At least ten thousand protesters were arrested and presumably punished harshly. China's reputation on the world stage took a serious hit.

Yet only a month later, a photo leaked out of U.S. national security adviser Brent Scowcroft's greeting Deng Xiaoping at a secret meeting in Beijing. Clearly the Bush administration wasn't going to punish the CCP over the massacre and suppression of the protesters. Despite the American public's widespread admiration for Tank Man and sympathy for the brave souls who built the Goddess of Democracy, our government quietly decided to look the other way at totalitarianism and human rights abuses. The Bush administration apparently decided that improving trade relations with the growing Chinese economy was more important.

When they were accused of putting capitalism ahead of promoting global freedom, some foreign policy experts argued that there was no need to choose between the two goals. They confidently predicted that rapid economic growth and increasing prosperity in China would naturally and inevitably lead to dramatic political liberalization. The idea of a booming capitalist economy under the control of an authoritarian regime was impossible to imagine, let alone prepare for.

Yet that was exactly the combination that Deng and the CCP set out to create. As we later learned from secret documents called the Tiananmen Papers, the main lesson they took from 1989 was the need to crack down even more tightly to prevent future protests. The CCP would have to be more vigilant about media control and indoctrination of the public, to prevent dangerous Western ideas like free speech, democracy, and human rights from seeping into China. And they would have to do so without losing the inflows of Western capital and technology that were essential to making China a world-class economic power. They would need a strong, unbreakable wall between politics and economics. As the internet emerged in the years ahead, that wall would have to include the "Great Firewall of China" to block the internet. Chinese citizens would have to be protected from dangerous Western websites and social networks, along with Western broadcasts and print media.

Since then, the CCP has suppressed any mention of the Tiananmen Square protests in Chinese media or classrooms. Even mentioning the events of 1989 is a crime. But China's leaders haven't forgotten the key lesson: Allowing the needs of the party to be seen as somehow distinct from the needs of the people would be catastrophic.

The other lesson was that the United States was the enemy of the CCP. More than an enemy, a direct threat to the party's survival. Whether true or not—and some have argued it was a terrible miscalculation—it was convenient. Blaming the United States for the Tiananmen protests distracted from the party's own problems with corruption and public dissension. To say that the United States had once again humiliated China fit the script of the hundred-year marathon. But now, China was no longer weak. Not strong yet, but able and eager to take on this enemy anyway it could. The New Cold War started in 1989. Except no one told us.

Reading the Book

In the following chapters, I'm going to excerpt key parts of *Unrestricted Warfare* and explain them. I've tried as much as possible to capture the writing style and ideas of the two literary colonels while paring down some long and sometimes confusing digressions. The book was translated from Mandarin Chinese by the U.S. government's Foreign Broadcast Information Service at the time of publication (it's still in the public domain and for sale on Amazon), so certain phrases become approximations. But overall, I think the colonels write clearly, and reading their own words—the words that have been read by a generation of Chinese military and political leaders—is the best way to absorb the ideas they are conveying. I've also tried to capture some of their flights of prose. Phrases such as "Technology is like 'magic shoes' on the feet of mankind" seem drawn more from ancient Chinese poetry than military doctrine.

The authors show a keen awareness of global events during a period of great upheaval, particularly in economics and technology, and do a good job of providing their own context. I've labeled from what parts of the book I'm excerpting and kept the actual chapters and subheadings. On occasion, I've interrupted the text with brackets to add facts and context where necessary.

I've tried to preserve the flow and flavor of their language, but cut out the redundancies and some of their more obscure theories. And then I explain the relevance and how the basic doctrine they develop foreshadows the actions we have seen coming from the Chinese Communist Party. I stress the CCP, because this is not an anti-Chinese book, but an anti-CCP book. Indeed, my hope is that if we confront the Communists with enough strength, China will change.

As you read, it's always important to remember that *UW* was published in 1999 and written in the year prior. It is both a look ahead and a look back. They are interpreting history and existing Chinese strategy and projecting into a world of technological developments. Their version of China, as I've noted, is not a global force yet but in the early stages of a growing economy that is soon to undergo an unprecedented boom. Western governments are pleased to see China beginning to prosper and become a good citizen in the global community. The Chinese leadership has other ideas.

CHAPTER 3

THE "MAGIC SHOES"
OF TECHNOLOGY

IN SEPTEMBER 2021, CHRISTOPHER WRAY, THE DIRECTOR of the Federal Bureau of Investigation, appeared before the U.S. Congress to discuss law enforcement threats to the United States. In his matter-of-fact way, he noted that there were more than two thousand ongoing investigations into Chinese espionage in the United States. "We're opening a new investigation that's tied back to China about every 12 hours, and it covers pretty much every sector of the economy in every state in the nation," Wray said. The colonels who wrote *Unrestricted Warfare* would be proud.

Their opening chapters make two key points: The United States is the enemy and the advance of technology is giving China the tools to defeat it. They see the United States as relying too much on technology from a *military* standpoint, and not understanding its uses in their proposed "new kind of war." And, of course, stealing that technology whenever possible becomes an essential task of warfare.

But technology is only the crack in the door for an under-resourced nation. It is a means to a much bigger end: the usurping of the United States. They have studied their enemy and found his weaknesses, which they begin to elaborate.

They see China as ideally suited to deal with these nonmilitary issues. For a democracy like the United States, the mission of a national military is to defend the homeland, its people, its allies, and its Constitution. But the People's Liberation Army is *not* a national military; it's the armed wing of the Chinese Communist Party. Its primary function—really its only function—is to keep the CCP in power. The needs of the Chinese people are much lower on the priority list, if they even appear at all.

This means that colonels like Qiao and Wang are, ultimately, political functionaries. Both from military families, they grew up in a system that sees warfare as entirely political. Their mission as PLA officers is to help the CCP impose its will on China's own civilians as well as on other countries. While these goals might be easier to achieve if the PLA could deploy superior weapons and troops, as the United States did when it imposed its will on Saddam Hussein and Slobodan Milošević, that's not essential anymore. They are describing a new kind of superpower that uses new ways to impose its will on others.

From the Preface of *Unrestricted Warfare*

Stalin ominously said, "When we hang the capitalists they will sell us the rope we use." Perhaps it was hyperbole, or perhaps Stalin just couldn't implement his vision.

... Who could imagine that an insufferably arrogant actor [the United States], *whose appearance has changed the entire plot, suddenly finds that he himself is actually the last person to play this unique role. Furthermore, without waiting for him to leave the stage, he has already been told that there is no great likelihood that he will again handle an A role, at least not a central role in which he alone occupies center stage. What kind of feeling would this be?*

Perhaps those who feel this most deeply are the Americans, who probably should be counted as among the few who want to play all the roles, including savior, fireman, world policeman, and an emissary of peace, etc.*

At a time when America might well have been at the peak of its global power, Qiao and Wang take a boldly counterintuitive approach—one that took hold and grew among the Chinese Communist leadership until it fully blossomed under Xi Jinping's assertions that the United States is a fading power. Despite acknowledging the masterful victory, Qiao and Wang believe that America's quick and overwhelming success in the Gulf War made the United States complacent and smug about its status as the world's only remaining military superpower. Their core idea is that this smugness created a huge opportunity for China to improve its global position through nonmilitary means. A decade of nearly uninterrupted American successes in the 1990s would plant the seeds for America's decline, which China could skillfully exploit.

The authors also argue that the Gulf War was the first domino

---

*Qiao Liang and Wang Xiangsui, *Unrestricted Warfare*, trans. Foreign Broadcast Information Service (Beijing: PLA Literature and Arts Publishing House, 1999), https://www.c4i.org/unrestricted.pdf.

of every major event that followed in the 1990s, including the final collapse of the Soviet Union and the Eastern European Communist states, the defeat of Milošević in Kosovo, and even the rise of the internet. They believe none of those events would have been possible without the hubris that followed the expulsion of Saddam Hussein's forces from Kuwait. Also worth noting is the colonels' description of America as an "insufferably arrogant actor." The rising generation of Chinese leaders, especially in the military, was building a deep resentment of the United States that has only grown to this day.

... In the aftermath of Desert Storm, Uncle Sam has not been able to again achieve a commendable victory. Whether it was in Somalia or Bosnia-Herzegovina, this has invariably been the case.... Faced with political, economic, cultural, diplomatic, ethnic, and religious issues that are more complex than they are in the minds of most of the military men in the world, the limitations of the military means, which had heretofore always been successful, suddenly became apparent.

However, in the age of "might makes right"—and most of the history of this century falls into this period—these were [nonmilitary] *issues which did not constitute a problem. The problem is that the U.S.-led multinational forces brought this period to a close in the desert region of Kuwait, thus beginning a new period.*

The authors mock the concept of America as the world's policeman, which was hotly debated among politicians, pundits, and scholars between the end of the Cold War and 9/11. When should the United States get involved in foreign conflicts, and when should it mind its own business? When should it defer to the United Nations, and when should it organize and lead its own coalitions of allies? And in an era of ethnic cleansing in Eastern Europe and attempted genocides in parts of Africa, how terrible did a human rights crisis have to get to justify American intervention?

None of these polarizing questions was definitively resolved by 1999, and as the authors predicted, they became increasingly irrelevant over the next two decades. When was the last time you heard a serious proposal for the U.S. military to act unilaterally to intervene in a dysfunctional foreign country? In the aftermath of our long post–9/11 entanglement in Afghanistan and Iraq, our appetite for nation building has essentially disappeared.

At present it is still hard to see if this age will lead to the unemployment of large numbers of military personnel, nor will it cause war to vanish from this world. All these are still undetermined. The only point which is certain is that, from this point on, war will no longer be what it was originally. Which is to say that, if in the days to come mankind has no choice but to engage in war, it can no longer be carried out in the ways with which we are familiar. . . .

When people begin to lean toward and rejoice in the reduced use of military force to resolve conflicts, war will be reborn in another form and in another arena, becoming an instrument of enormous power in the hands of all those who harbor intentions of controlling other countries or regions. . . .

The financial attack by George Soros on East Asia [billionaire investor Soros is repeatedly cited as a destructive financial manipulator], *the terrorist attack on the U.S. embassy by Usama Bin Laden* [they make many eerily prescient references to bin Laden], *the gas attack on the Tokyo subway by the disciples of the Aum Shinri Kyo, and the havoc wreaked by the likes of Morris Jr. on the Internet*

[Robert Morris, a grad student who created one of the first viral computer worms], *in which the degree of destruction is by no means second to that of a war, represent semi-warfare, quasi-warfare, and sub-warfare, that is, the embryonic form of another kind of warfare.*

But whatever you call them, they cannot make us more optimistic than in the past. We have no reason for optimism. This is because the reduction of the functions of warfare in a pure sense does not mean at all that war has ended. Even in the so-called post-modern, post-industrial age, warfare will not be totally dismantled. It has only re-invaded human society in a more complex, more extensive, more concealed, and more subtle manner. . . . While we are seeing a relative reduction in military violence, at the same time we definitely are see-ing an increase in political, economic, and technological violence. However, regardless of the form the violence takes, war is war, and a change in the external appearance does not keep any war from abid-ing by the principles of war.

If we acknowledge that the new principles of war are no longer "using armed force to compel the enemy to submit to one's will," but rather are "using all means, including armed force or non-armed force, military and non-military, and lethal and non-lethal means to compel the enemy to accept one's interests."

This represents change. A change in war and a change in the mode of war occasioned by this. So, just what has led to the change? What kind of changes are they? Where are the changes headed? How does one face these changes? This is the topic that this book attempts to touch on and shed light on, and it is also our motivation in deciding to write this book.

Qiao and Wang are previewing the heart of their argument: the rise of a total, unrestricted type of warfare that will include every resource at the CCP's disposal—economic, diplomatic, technological, and more. They're reassuring the party that America can no longer impose its will on the rest of the world via military domination. Nuclear war is unthinkable, land warfare is increasingly unpopular, and America's preferred use of force—strategic bombing—isn't enough to crush a determined civilian population that supports its government. We've seen that repeatedly from World War II (including both the Nazi Blitz against the United Kingdom and the Allied air raids against Germany) to Vietnam. This is partly why Mao's "people's war" against Chiang Kai-shek focused on persuading the Chinese people to lose faith in the nationalist government and embrace the Communist revolution. Popular opinion can't be changed through military power alone, but effective propaganda and indoctrination can steer hearts and minds. And so much of that work depends on controlling and dominating the forces of technology—if you use them properly.

Introduction to Part One

TECHNOLOGY IS THE TOTEM OF MODERN MAN

... Technology has achieved startling and explosive developments in a rather short period of time, and this has resulted in innumerable benefits for mankind, which is anxious for quick success and instant rewards.... Technology is like "magic shoes" on the feet of mankind, and

*after the spring has been wound tightly by commercial interests, peo-
ple can only dance along with the shoes, whirling rapidly in time to
the beat that they set....*

*There is absolutely no doubt that the appearance of information
technology has been good news for human civilization.... It is just
that, at present, there is still a question of who in turn will have a magic
charm with which to control it. The pessimistic viewpoint is that, if
this technology develops in a direction which cannot be controlled by
man, ultimately it will turn mankind into its victim....*

*Over the past 300 years, people have long since become accus-
tomed to blindly falling in love with the new and discarding the old in
the realm of technology, and the endless pursuit of new technology
has become a panacea to resolve all the difficult questions of existence. Infatuated with it, people have gradually gone astray....*

*Fortunately, at this time, modern information technology made
its appearance. We can say with certainty that this is the most important revolution in the history of technology. Its revolutionary significance is not merely in that it is a brand new technology itself, but more
in that it is a kind of bonding agent which can lightly penetrate the
layers of barriers between technologies and link various technologies
which appear to be totally unrelated.... The emergence of information
technology has presented endless possibilities for matchups involving
various old and new technologies.... The general fusion of technology
is irreversibly guiding the rising globalization trend, while the globalization trend in turn is accelerating the process of the general fusion
of technology, and this is the basic characteristic of our age.*

*This characteristic will inevitably project its features on every di-
rection of the age, and naturally the realm of war will be no exception.*

No military force that thirsts for modernization can get by without nurturing new technology, while the demands of war have always been the midwife of new technology. During the Gulf War, more than 500 kinds of new and advanced technology of the 80s ascended the stage to strike a pose, making the war simply seem like a demonstration site for new weaponry. However, the thing that left a profound impression on people was not the new weaponry per se, but rather the trend of systemization in the development and use of the weapons. . . . The real-time coordination of numerous weapons over great distances created an unprecedented combat capability, unimaginable prior to the emergence of information technology. . . .

War in the age of technological integration and globalization has eliminated the right of weapons to label war and, with regard to the new starting point, has realigned the relationship of weapons to war, while the appearance of weapons of new concepts, and particularly new concepts of weapons, has gradually blurred the face of war. Does a single "hacker" attack count as a hostile act or not? Can using financial instruments to destroy a country's economy be seen as a battle? Did CNN's broadcast of an exposed corpse of a U.S. soldier in the streets of Mogadishu shake the determination of the Americans to act as the world's policeman, thereby altering the world's strategic situation? And should an assessment of wartime actions look at the means or the results? Obviously, proceeding with the traditional definition of war in mind, there is no longer any way to answer the above questions. When we suddenly realize that all these non-war actions may be the new factors constituting future warfare, we have to come up with a new name for this new form of war: Warfare which transcends all boundaries and limits. In short: unrestricted warfare.

If this name becomes established, this kind of war means that all means will be in readiness, that information will be omnipresent, and the battlefield will be everywhere. It means that all weapons and technology can be superimposed at will, it means that all the boundaries lying between the two worlds of war and non-war, of military and non-military, will be totally destroyed, and it also means that many of the current principles of combat will be modified, and even that the rules of war may need to be rewritten.

They have quickly framed their title and thesis: the ability, and necessity, to wage unrestricted warfare. And their path to that insight was an early-stage understanding about the opportunities and limits of technology.

The authors compare Western fascination with technology in general to the "magic shoes" of Hans Christian Andersen's fairy tale—he actually titled it "The Red Shoes"—because the products of Silicon Valley will end up controlling us more than we control them. Qiao and Wang are warning about a future of runaway information technology that can no longer be controlled by the smart people who created it. They see information technology, especially the internet, as a threat to the CCP's ability to define reality for the Chinese people. Their alarm will soon lead to the creation of the Great Firewall of China—a high-tech solution to keeping the unrestricted internet from bringing in dangerous ideas like freedom and democracy.

Furthermore, they see the internet as such a serious threat to the party that it demands a response from the People's Liberation Army, not just from Chinese technologists. It's as urgent to them as a mobilization of enemy troops on the border. Unfiltered information pouring into China would allow people to escape the party's carefully constructed information bubble, creating an existential risk to the entire regime.

Of course, the PLA's strategic thinking couldn't be more different from the mindset taught to American military officers. While these two Chinese colonels were writing *UW*, I was a young captain at Minot Air Force Base, training for combat missions as a B-52 pilot. I was never told to think of the information flow to civilians as an aspect of national security. And I was taught that the needs of any political party are irrelevant to the mission of a military officer, because politics and the military are completely separate spheres.

They are further stressing that the internet and related infotech are fundamentally different from previous waves of technology. For all the hype about the web in the United States during the dot-com bubble, these Chinese observers might have seen it more clearly than any American pundit. They were right that the trends toward global free trade and global free information would naturally reinforce each other in a never-ending cycle, if left unchecked. Not everyone foresaw what they called "the basic characteristic of our age"—technology driving globalization and then globalization accelerating more technology. While American investors focused on the web's potential to transform business, the colonels focused on its potential to transform war.

When the colonels state that the face of war has "blurred," they mean that we can no longer define war by the types of weapons being used. We will never again have the simple labels for eras of warfare, like the ages of the longbow, or gunpowder, or the tank, or the atomic bomb. Future wars will be dramatically different, and the old proverb that generals tend to plan for the previous war has never been more relevant.

The colonels recognized the media's ability to "shake the determination of the Americans" and shift national consensus. During the 1990s, CNN's satellite hookups beamed images of atrocities against U.S. troops, like the Mogadishu incident, into every American living room. Those images damaged public support for President Clinton's intervention in Somalia. The flow of information had a direct impact on U.S. policy, forcing a pullback from the course it would have taken without those CNN satellites.

"The battlefield will be everywhere" is the heart of *UW*'s thesis. The West could have and should have understood the military implications of the technological shifts of the 1990s, but we were oblivious. Building on the ancient Chinese traditions of victory without war, the authors saw that global television and the internet would rewrite the rules of war, opening creative options for unrestricted warfare, from computer hacking to media manipulation.

Their suggestion to modify "the current principles of war" is much more than a simple shift in tactics, as had happened many times across military history. For instance, George Washington's forces during the Revolutionary War introduced guerrilla warfare against lined formations, and war was never the same after that. But the concept of unrestricted warfare goes much further, changing the definition of *who* fights and bringing civilians irrevocably into the battle.

Today, why not replicate the Mogadishu incident by moving some of your own civilians into war zones whenever a Western power was planning airstrikes? That would lead to CNN and the internet spreading images of slaughtered innocents. International outrage and condemnation would almost certainly fall on the military force that dropped the bombs on those civilians, not the cold-blooded government that put them in the line of fire to trigger atrocities. The result would be a huge, asymmetric advantage for any ruthless country willing to throw out the Geneva Conventions and other standards of ethical warfare.

American military strategists and political leaders were nowhere close to this analysis in 1999—in fact, they're still resisting it two decades later. Recent books like *The Kill Chain* by Christian Brose are still focused on making our military more effective at blowing things up, using cutting-edge technology to identify and hit targets more accurately and quickly. But this approach misses the point. Efficiency doesn't matter if the real war is being conducted without blowing anyone up. In 2021, we still lack the clarity and insight that the authors of *UW* had in 1999.

So much of the power of technology is tied to information and the question of who controls that information. The most sophisticated generals have always understood the importance of information in warfare. It's often said that truth is the first casualty of war, and even democratic societies have sometimes lied to the public, such as the United States in both world wars. But democracy is so far not the Chinese way and harsh control of the media has been a hallmark of the CCP, starting with the Great Firewall. Launched in the wake of *Unrestricted Warfare,* the firewall is meant to block almost all Western media, particularly internet sources such as Google and Facebook, as well as news providers such as *The New York Times* and *The Washington Post*.

That desire for control has led to the creation of a literal army of Chinese citizens engaged in cyberwar, policing the internet, creating false propaganda on social media, and stealing the next generation of technology. As discussed in the next chapter, all this and more are weapons of war. And weapons the United States has conveniently ignored for many years.

CHAPTER 4

THE WEAPONS REVOLUTION

IN JANUARY 2018, MARRIOTT INTERNATIONAL, THE GIANT hotel chain, fired an employee named Roy Jones. An American social media manager for Marriott, he had "liked" a Tweet from a Tibetan independence group that seemed to imply that Tibet was separate from China. Someone in the Shanghai tourism bureau, spotted Jones's Tweet and reported it to the CCP. For the thought crime of liking the Tweet, the CCP expressed its outrage to Marriott, which manages many hotels in China. Marriott fired Jones.

A bizarrely petty move, one might think, but also an important one, because it gives us a glimpse of China acting on an idea from Chapter 1 of *Unrestricted Warfare*. China was able to control a massive corporation's behavior outside of China by using what President Xi Jinping calls his "magic weapon": the use of information technology along with China's primary resource: people (and because Marriott owns hotels in China).

For thousands of years, up through the nuclear age, humans have labeled eras of warfare according to the dominant weapons technology of the time. But the new concept of unrestricted warfare makes that kind of language obsolete. We can't even call this the nuclear age anymore, as Qiao and Wang will explain shortly. It's time to fundamentally rethink warfare, and while naming conventions might seem trivial, names greatly affect how we process new ideas.

In 1998, when *Unrestricted Warfare* was written, China did not have stealth bombers or an adequate navy. But in the view of the colonels, it had many weapons: It had more than a billion people. It had computer programmers and devious hackers pouring out of universities each year. It had financial speculators and currency reserves. It had doctors studying lethal viruses. All, and more, should be considered weapons. While their enemies would be spending money on guns, China would be buying and building computer chips—and everything else.

The ships and planes of other nations, worth hundreds of billions of dollars and needing constant upgrades, were meant to fight the last war. What China has is suited to the next one.

In this chapter, we'll look at how the colonels recommend the weaponizing of everything. We'll look at their belief that swollen military budgets are actually destructive to the spender. And we'll consider what to make of China's current explosion of military spending, considering the strategy they've held to date. Does this insight allow us to glimpse a change in strategy? Is China girding for a conventional conflict? Or is this a Potemkin ruse to goad the United States into spending more?

The colonels also focus on another kind of weapon: a commercial airliner. Written before the 9/11 attacks, the colonels nonetheless predict something like that will occur. They write: *Everything that can benefit mankind can also harm him. This is to say that there is nothing in the world today that cannot become a weapon.* Such as a commercial jetliner loaded with fuel.

From Chapter 1 of *Unrestricted Warfare*

The weapons revolution invariably precedes the revolution in military affairs by one step, and following the arrival of a revolutionary weapon, the arrival of a revolution in military affairs is just a matter of time. The history of warfare is continually providing this kind of proof: bronze or iron spears resulted in the infantry phalanx; bows and arrows and stirrups provided new tactics for cavalry. Black powder cannons gave rise to a full complement of modern warfare modes. . . . *From the time when conical bullets and rifles took to the battlefield as the vanguard of the age of technology, weapons straightaway stamped their names on the chest of warfare.*

First, it was the enormous steel-clad naval vessels that ruled the seas, launching the "age of battleships," then its brother the "tank" ruled land warfare, after which the airplane dominated the skies, up until the atomic bomb was born, announcing the approach of the "nuclear age." Today, a multitude of new and advanced technology weapons continues to pour forth. . . . [People are] *calling it "electronic warfare," "precision-weapons warfare," and "information warfare." Coasting along in their mental orbit, people have not yet noticed that a certain inconspicuous yet very important change is stealthily approaching.*

The authors are urging readers to make a fundamental shift in mindset about how we think about war.

NO ONE HAS THE RIGHT TO LABEL WARFARE

... What is different than in the past is that the revolution in military affairs that is coming will no longer be driven by one or two individual weapons. ... In the past, all that was needed was the invention of a few weapons or pieces of equipment, such as the stirrup and the Maxim machine gun, and that was sufficient to alter the form of war, whereas today upwards of 100 kinds of weapons are needed to make up a certain weapons system before it can have an overall effect on war. However, the more weapons that are invented, the smaller any individual weapon's role in war becomes, and this is a paradox that is inherent in the relationship between weapons and war. ... Other than the all-out use of nuclear weapons, a situation which is more and more unlikely and which may be termed nuclear war, none of the other weapons, even those that are extremely revolutionary in nature, possesses the right to label future warfare. ...

High technology, as spoken of in generalities, cannot become a synonym for future warfare, nor is information technology ... sufficient to name a war. Even if in future wars all the weapons have information components embedded in them and are fully computerized, we can still not term such war "information warfare" ... because, regardless of how important information technology is, it cannot completely supplant the functions and roles of each technology per se. For example, the F-22 fighter, which already fully embodies information technology, is still a fighter, and the "Tomahawk" missile is still a missile, and one cannot lump them all together as "information weapons," nor can a war that's conducted using these weapons be termed information warfare. Computerized warfare in the broad sense and information warfare in the narrow sense are two completely different things. The former refers to the various forms of warfare which are enhanced and accompanied by information technology, while the latter primarily refers to war in which information technology is used to obtain or suppress information. . . .

We are by no means denying that, in future warfare, certain advanced weapons may play a leading role. However, as for determining the outcome of war, it is now very difficult for anyone to occupy an unmatched position. It may be leading, but it will not be alone, much less never-changing.

Many American military and civilian leaders—especially Donald Rumsfeld, the secretary of defense during the post–9/11 wars in Iraq and Afghanistan—focused on constantly improving our weapons systems in terms of accuracy and lethality. Rumsfeld called this approach the Revolution in Military Affairs (RMA), and he considered its implementation one of his major accomplishments at the Pentagon. He was obsessed with using technology to speed up every military process, making every response to every military threat more efficient.

But Qiao and Wang considered our huge investments in cutting-edge weapons to be a misallocation of resources and a dangerous distraction from what really matters in international conflicts. Historically, of course, it mattered tremendously which country had the fastest ships, the most accurate cannons, the bombers with the longest flying range. But the authors saw the approach of a new era in which those metrics were less and less important. For instance, it doesn't matter how fast, deadly, and high-tech your F-22s are if the greatest threat to America isn't coming by air at all.

It's important to remember that *UW* was written more than two years before 9/11, when Al Qaeda seriously damaged the United States with the lowest of low-tech weapons: nineteen men armed with nothing but box cutters and their resolve to die for jihad. All the billions of Pentagon spending on cutting-edge systems couldn't stop that unconventional threat. After the initial and brilliantly unconventional defeat of the Taliban by U.S. special ops and their local allies in the early 2000s, things quickly became conventional and it took many years and many more billions of dollars to merely block the vastly underpowered forces of the Taliban in Afghanistan— efforts that became too costly in blood and treasure to sustain. In Iraq, the application of swift and overwhelming conventional forces—an upgraded version of the first Gulf War—failed to kill an insurgency that erupted into a brutal guerrilla war that cost thousands of U.S. lives and hundreds of billions of dollars in return for a tenuous peace. The estimated cost of both those post–9/11 actions is estimated north of $2 trillion; some would argue it may be double that.

From the CCP's perspective, the shift predicted by *UW* and confirmed on and after 9/11 was great news. China didn't have a fighter jet even remotely as advanced as the F-22, but that didn't matter, because we're not in the age of the fighter jet anymore. And

China could become far, far better at unconventional warfare than an old-fashioned dictatorship like that of Saddam Hussein.

"FIGHTING THE FIGHT THAT FITS ONE'S WEAPONS" AND "MAKING THE WEAPONS TO FIT THE FIGHT"

. . . In the history of war, the general unwritten rule that people have adhered to all along is to "fight the fight that fits one's weapons." Very often it is the case that only after one first has a weapon does one begin to formulate tactics to match it. With weapons coming first, followed by tactics, the evolution of weapons has a decisive constraining effect on the evolution of tactics. . . .

Today, those engaged in warfare . . . hardly realize that the United States, the foremost power in the world, must similarly face this kind of helplessness. Even though she is the richest in the world, it is not necessarily possible for her to use up her uniform new and advanced technology weapons to fight an expensive modern war. . . .

If one thinks that one must rely on advanced weapons to fight a modern war, being blindly superstitious about the miraculous effects of such weapons, it may actually result in turning something miraculous into something rotten. . . .

[But] the position of weapons in invariably preceding a revolution in military affairs has now been shaken, and now tactics come first, and weapons follow, or the two encourage one another, with advancement in a push-pull manner becoming the new relationship between them. . . . Customizing weapons systems to tactics that are still being explored and studied is like preparing food for a great banquet without

knowing who is coming, where the slightest error can lead one far astray. Viewed from the performance of the U.S. military in Somalia, where they were at a loss when they encountered Aidid's forces [the ragged gunmen of warlord Mohammed Aidid, who tried to force foreign troops out of Somalia in the early 1990s], *the most modern military force does not have the ability to control public clamor, and cannot deal with an opponent who does things in an unconventional manner. On the battlefields of the future, the digitized forces may very possibly be like a great cook who is good at cooking lobsters sprinkled with butter, when faced with guerrillas who resolutely gnaw corncobs, they can only sigh in despair. . . . Looking at the specific examples of battles that we have, it is difficult for high-tech troops to deal with unconventional warfare and low-tech warfare. . . .*

The authors were right in this diagnosis: For the first time in history, unilateral access to superior weapons technology stopped conferring a big advantage to the dominant power. America's enormous nuclear arsenal would be useless in small-scale deployments like Somalia in the 1990s, or in the counterinsurgency campaigns in Afghanistan and Iraq in the 2000s. Likewise with all of our cutting-edge conventional weapons, developed and deployed at huge expense as part of Rumsfeld's Revolution in Military Affairs. "Helplessness" is a strong word, but not much of an exaggeration. We thought we were strong by having the world's most advanced weaponry, but we found ourselves in situations where it was impossible to fight with the full power of our weapons, or anywhere close to it. And we fell catastrophically behind in making the weapons we actually did need for the fights we got into, such as effective counterinsurgency strategies.

I remember rereading this section in dismay at the Pentagon in 2014. It crystallized so many problems we had been having since the late 1990s and how badly we had misplayed the evolution of international conflict. I became determined to warn as many people as possible.

WEAPONS OF NEW CONCEPTS AND
NEW CONCEPTS OF WEAPONS

. . . All these weapons and weapons platforms that have been produced in line with traditional thinking have without exception come to a dead end in their efforts to adapt to modern warfare and future warfare. Those desires of using the magic of high-technology to work some alchemy on traditional weapons so that they are completely remade have ultimately fallen into the high-tech trap involving the endless waste of limited funds and an arms race. This is the paradox that must inevitably be faced in the process of the development of traditional weapons: To ensure that the weapons are in the lead, one must continue to up the ante in development costs; the result of this continued raising of the stakes is that no one has enough money to maintain the lead. Its ultimate result is that the weapons to defend the country actually become a cause of national bankruptcy.

Perhaps the most recent examples are the most convincing. Marshal Orgakov [sic], *the former chief of the Soviet general staff* [Nikolai Ogarkov was chief of staff from 1977 to 1984], *was acutely aware of the trend of weapons development in the "nuclear age," and when, at an opportune time, he proposed the brand-new concept of the "revolution in military technology," his thinking was clearly ahead of those of his generation. But being ahead of time in his thinking hardly brought his country happiness, and actually brought about disastrous results. As soon as this concept . . . was proposed, it further intensified the arms race which had been going on for some time between the United States and the Soviet Union. It was just that, at that time no one could predict that it would actually result in the breakup of the Soviet Union and its complete elimination from the superpower contest. A powerful empire collapsed without a single shot being fired, vividly corroborating the lines of the famous poem by Kipling, "When empires perish, it is not with a rumble, but a snicker." Not only was this true for the former Soviet Union, today the Americans seem to be following in the footsteps of their old adversary, providing fresh proof of the paradox of weapons development that we have proposed. As the outlines of the age of technology integration become increasingly clear, they are investing more and more in the development of new weapons, and the cost of the weapons is getting higher and higher. . . .*

If this is still true for the rich and brash United States, then how far can the other countries, who are short of money, continue down this path? Obviously, it will be difficult for anyone to keep going. Naturally, the way to extricate oneself from this predicament is to develop a different approach. . . .

However, the Americans have not been able to get their act together in this area. This is because proposing a new concept of weapons does not require relying on the springboard of new technology, it just demands lucid and incisive thinking. However, this is not a strong point of the Americans, who are slaves to technology in their thinking. The Americans invariably halt their thinking at the boundary where technology has not yet reached. It cannot be denied that man-made earthquakes, tsunamis, weather disasters, or subsonic wave and new biological and chemical weapons all constitute new concept weapons, and that they have tremendous differences with what we normally speak of as weapons, but they are still all weapons whose immediate goal is to kill and destroy, and which are still related to military af- fairs, soldiers, and munitions. Speaking in this sense, they are nothing more than non-traditional weapons whose mechanisms have been altered and whose lethal power and destructive capabilities have been magnified several times over.

However, a new concept of weapons is different. . . . Everything that can benefit mankind can also harm him. This is to say that there is nothing in the world today that cannot become a weapon, and this requires that our understanding of weapons must have an awareness that breaks through all boundaries. With technological developments being in the process of striving to increase the types of weapons, a breakthrough in our thinking can open up the domain of the weapons kingdom at one stroke. As we see it, a single man-made stock-market crash, a single computer virus invasion, or a single rumor or scandal that results in a fluctuation in the enemy country's exchange rates or exposes the leaders of an enemy country on the Internet, all can be included in the ranks of new-concept weapons. . . .

What must be made clear is that the new concept of weapons is in the process of creating weapons that are closely linked to the lives of the common people. . . . The new concept of weapons will cause ordinary people and military men alike to be greatly aston- ished at the fact that commonplace things that are close to them can also become weapons with which to engage in war. We believe that some morning people will awake to discover with surprise that quite a few gentle and kind things have begun to have offensive and lethal characteristics.

In this section they're almost gloating about the misallocation of America's defense budget, which was $298 billion in 1999 and ballooned to north of $700 billion by 2020. We're spending ourselves into an unfathomable national debt while simultaneously failing to address the greatest threat to our national security—the CCP's stealth war in its relentless drive to dominate the world.

The authors see a cautionary tale in the fall of the Soviet Union in the late 1980s, in large part because of its overspending on cutting-edge weapons systems, especially the nuclear arms race against the United States. As they note, the Cold War ended without a shot being fired. It would be the ultimate irony if the United States also lost its superpower status by massively overspending on advanced weapons that were ineffective against a nuclear-armed rival while ignoring our crumbling infrastructure and other urgent national needs. Meanwhile, the CCP has been focusing its resources not on an arms race but on building China's infrastructure and manufacturing capacity, and on reinforcing the Great Firewall that blocks the outside world from interfering with the totalitarian regime's control of its own citizens.

They're also mocking Americans as "slaves to technology" who can't bring themselves to even imagine, let alone execute, the kind of stealth war strategy for international conflict that China has developed. The colonels claim that if a weapon isn't high-tech and expensive, Americans can't even recognize it as a weapon, despite the obvious truth that "everything that can benefit mankind can also harm him."

This is their key point: the urgency of weaponizing virtually any aspect of daily life, from the global financial markets to the way our media (and now, social media) can spread disinformation. There's no need to resort to biological or chemical warfare or setting off a man-made earthquake—whatever that might have been, there were no details provided. Those kinds of direct attacks on civilians would trigger a devastating conventional military response from the United States. The CCP would get so much further by being creative in new ways to cause havoc, literally under the radar.

The reference to less wealthy nations is also a reminder that while the United States is Enemy No. 1, China has multiple potential adversaries. *How far can the other countries, who are short of money, continue down this path?* reflects their awareness of wary Asian neighbors with whom they have clashed in the past, such as Japan, India, Vietnam—and of course Taiwan.

Interestingly, in the next section they make a rare acknowledgment of international law and the notion of "crime against mankind"—precepts of the civilized world that do not much trouble them elsewhere in the book. They seem to say that once they've taken nuclear war or some kind of massive bombardment off the table, all other means of destroying a society are legitimate.

THE TREND TO "KINDER" WEAPONS

... Philosophical principles tell us that, whenever something reaches an ultimate point, it will turn in the opposite direction. The invention of nuclear weapons, this "ultra-lethal weapon" which can wipe out all mankind, has plunged mankind into an existential trap of its own

making. Nuclear weapons have become a sword of Damocles hanging over the head of mankind, which forces it to ponder: Do we really need "ultra-lethal" weapons? What is the difference between killing an enemy once and killing him 100 times? What is the point of defeating the enemy if it means risking the destruction of the world? How do we avoid warfare that results in ruin for all? . . .

The "Universal Declaration of Human Rights" passed by the United Nations General Assembly in 1948, and more than 50 subsequent pacts related to it, have established a set of international rules for human rights in which it is recognized that the use of weapons of mass destruction—particularly nuclear weapons—is a serious violation of the "right to life" and represents a "crime against mankind." . . .

The trend to "kinder" weapons is nothing other than a reflection in the production and development of weapons of this great change in man's cultural background. At the same time, technological progress has given us the means to strike at the enemy's nerve center directly without harming other things, giving us numerous new options for achieving victory, and all these make people believe that the best way to achieve victory is to control, not to kill. There have been changes in the concept of war and the concept of weapons, and the approach of using uncontrolled slaughter to force the enemy into unconditional surrender has now become the relic of a bygone age. . . .

The appearance of precision-kill (accurate) weapons and non-lethal (non-fatal) weapons is a turning point in the development of weapons, showing for the first time that weapons are developing in a "kinder," not a "stronger" direction. Precision-kill weapons can hit a target precisely, reducing collateral casualties, and like a gamma knife which can excise a tumor with hardly any bleeding, it has led to "surgical" strikes and other such new tactics, so that inconspicuous combat actions can achieve extremely notable strategic results....

Non-lethal weapons can effectively eliminate the combat capabilities of personnel and equipment without loss of life. The trend that is embodied in these weapons shows that mankind is in the process of overcoming its own extreme thinking, beginning to learn to control the lethal power that it already has but which is increasingly excessive. In the massive bombing that lasted more than a month during the Gulf War, the loss of life among civilians in Iraq only numbered in the thousands, far less than in the massive bombing of Dresden during World War II.

Nuclear weapons aren't going away, and indeed more countries than ever either have them or are trying to develop them. But for a superpower like the United States, their only real value now is as a deterrent. China understood this early on and mostly stayed out of the nuclear arms race during the Cold War. Until recently, the CCP chose to maintain a minimal nuclear arsenal, just enough to deter any other nation's potential nuclear strike. By keeping its stockpile modest and its nuclear budget limited, the Chinese avoided the massive expenses that helped bring down the Soviet Union. As their wealth has grown, the Chinese have added to their nuclear stockpile, creating alarm and some confusion among Western analysts. Are new silos and warheads just a deepening of their deterrence force, or is this a change of strategy in creating an offensive nuclear capability? Is it perhaps a ruse, with empty silos or hollow missiles meant to provoke the United States and others to waste yet more billions? From the colonels' perspective in 1998, nuclear war is obsolete, but this may be an area where the Chinese leadership has moved beyond that notion. And even if they are simply increasing their deterrence, does that mean we have to increase our lethality?

This is a key point that America's military establishment still hasn't grappled with. We haven't seen nuclear weapons used in warfare since 1945, which is great news for humanity, but a financial drag on a country that continues to invest billions in ever more powerful and sophisticated nukes. Beyond a minimum level of deterrence, developing extra lethality that will effectively destroy the world is a waste of resources. The same is true for what the authors call "ultra-lethal" conventional weapons.

Even one of today's most respected military strategists, former Marine general and former secretary of defense James Mattis, has a blind spot regarding lethality—the sheer destructive potential of a military force. During his time running the Department of Defense, Mattis focused on making our armed forces more efficient at killing future enemies in a future conventional war. The entire Pentagon fell in line with that way of thinking, in part by reading books about efficient lethality like *The Kill Chain,* which I mentioned in the previous chapter. Our top leaders have focused on deploying the latest Silicon Valley technology to get better at what the military already does without stopping to reconsider if our military should pivot to very different priorities.

It's not hard to see how these ideas get locked in. Imagine being the world's best typewriter repairman and so concentrated on the demands of your craft that you miss the transition to PCs and word processing. By the time you figure out that your hard-won mastery is nearly obsolete, you might already be out of business. It has nothing to do with intelligence—Mattis and other Pentagon leaders were extremely smart. The problem is losing sight of the fundamental purpose of having a military.

Qiao and Wang were prescient about this trend toward precision strikes that avoid escalating into war. Look at how the Trump administration took out Iranian general Qasem Soleimani in January 2020, without triggering a much-feared military conflict. We've gotten better and better at assassinating a single enemy leader from the air, which is the exact opposite approach of carpet bombing that inflicts heavy civilian casualties. This can be a very effective way to take out an enemy like Soleimani, who was directly responsible for a significant number of American deaths. There was no need to kill thousands of Iranian troops, let alone civilians, as collateral damage.

They hint at other futuristic concepts that have come to reality:

Today, we already have enough technology, and we can create many methods of causing fear which are more effective, such as using a laser beam to project the image of injured followers against the sky, which would be sufficient to frighten those soldiers who are devoutly religious. There are no longer any obstacles to building this kind of weapon; it just requires that some additional imagination be added to the technical element. . . .

Information weapons are a prominent example of kinder weapons. Whether it involves electromagnetic energy weapons for hard destruction or soft-strikes by computer logic bombs, network viruses, or media weapons, all are focused on paralyzing and undermining, not personnel casualties.

Kinder weapons, which could only be born in an age of technical integration, may very well be the most promising development trend for weapons, and at the same time they will bring about forms of war or revolutions in military affairs which we cannot imagine or predict today. . . . Nonetheless, we still cannot indulge in romantic fantasies about technology, believing that from this point on war will become a confrontation like an electronic game, and even simulated warfare in a computer room similarly must be premised upon a country's actual overall capabilities, and if a colossus with feet of clay comes up with ten plans for simulated warfare, it will still not be sufficient to deter an enemy who is more powerful with regard to actual strength.

War is still the ground of death and life, the path of survival and destruction, and even the slightest innocence is not tolerated. Even if some day all the weapons have been made completely humane, a kinder war in which bloodshed may be avoided is still war. It may alter the cruel process of war, but there is no way to change the essence of war, which is one of compulsion, and therefore it cannot alter its cruel outcome, either.

The colonels are warning the CCP leadership not to get complacent about the potential of high-tech "kinder" weapons in isolation. No matter how precise targeting technology becomes, kinder weapons won't be sufficient to achieve the CCP's goals or avoid drawing a conventional military response from their enemies. This is another argument for pursuing unconventional and unrestricted warfare. The authors see the invention of those precise, less indiscriminate weapons as paving the way for even more creative uses of modern technology to redefine war, far beyond the traditional battlefield. A bloodless war—a stealth war—can do much more to achieve the CCP's goals than even the best military equipment on Earth.

I remember having a hard time wrapping my head around this chapter when I first encountered it. As an Air Force officer, I was taught that there's a clear separation between politics and the military. Politicians negotiate peace, and generals manage war. Either Congress issues a declaration of war or a president orders an official use of military force. We were taught that those boundaries were crucial and fundamental.

But now we're facing an enemy that not only ignores those boundaries but doesn't even frame the question that way. The authors are right that war has been increasingly decoupled from bloodshed, to a far more complete degree than the less bloody options of "kinder weapons." A country being attacked in an unrestricted war might not even realize that it has been attacked—whereas the Iranians absolutely knew they were being attacked in January 2020, even with just a single casualty.

But while the colonels keenly foresee the tools of "kinder war," they don't extrapolate the potential consequences. A disruption of a nation's electric grid or gasoline pipeline may be "bloodless" at the outset, but the resultant chaos is anything but benign.

Still, the phrase that rings out and tells us so much about China's strategy—as seen in the "magic weapon" work of the millions of individuals hired as subcontractors and referred to as United Front soldiers—was this: *The best way to achieve victory is to control, not to kill.*

CHAPTER 5

THE WAR GOD'S FACE HAS BECOME INDISTINCT

WHEN I WORKED IN THE WHITE HOUSE FOR THE NATIONAL Security Council, I asked the acting director of the Office of National Drug Control Policy what he was doing about the tens of thousands of Americans who were dying from overdoses of fentanyl, which is often smuggled in from China. He said, "We're cooperating with the Chinese government to bring the makers of the drugs to justice." I told him the CCP was not really cooperating with him, no matter what they told him. In fact, they were either directly or indirectly behind the drug smuggling. His response was total disbelief, claiming that Chinese law enforcement had recently arrested some producers of fentanyl. I said those producers would soon be out of prison and back in business. As long as they were selling only to the United States, the CCP didn't care about illegal drug sales or American overdoses. I also told him that Chinese pharmaceutical factories that made drugs legally for major American brands were certainly involved. He still didn't buy it.

I thought of that conversation as I studied this chapter of *UW*.

It brings together the immorality of the CCP and the naivete of the America government. War with no rules means just that. Nothing is out of bounds. A plague of drug deaths makes a good propaganda point about a decaying society.

This comprehensive chapter swiftly takes us through a history of war, a history of China, the evolution of the colonels' theory of unrestricted war, how that war blurs the lines between military and civilians, and a very specific list of the kind of war they envision. They write lyrically about the past and with an unemotional directness about the future. Here we find one of the book's most concise and disturbing quotes:

Just think, if it's even possible to start a war in a computer room or a stock exchange that will send an enemy country to its doom, then is there non-battlespace anywhere?

If that young lad setting out with his orders should ask today: "Where is the battlefield?" The answer would be: "Everywhere."

The United States simply doesn't see it that way. We are siloed into military—which is mostly set up to fight battles—and a giant bureaucracy, which deals with China on a piecemeal basis, assuming they are dealing with equally earnest bureaucrats trying to solve a problem. The Chinese counterpart has different assumptions because he too is a soldier. Which is why we should not trust any part of their government.

When I would brief our senior military leaders about the stealth war they had two responses: "Holy shit!" and "That's not my job."

The roots of Chinese history—both the military tactics and the country's sense of lost greatness, humiliation by the West, and the yearning for restoration—are important underlying themes that help give the book its power. The colonels are, to a great extent, preaching to the choir. Their vision is not a radical departure from centuries of Chinese beliefs but rather a modernized and practical version, distilled over three decades of Communist propaganda.

For those who are reassured that China is not a historically warlike nation—based on a lack of imperial conquests—history shows that there remain deep veins of warrior culture and military tradition. The Chinese have fought many wars within their own vast borders. But although there was plenty of bloodshed, the notion of a war without violence recurs in much Chinese thought, most notably in *The Art of War*. Mao's *Little Red Book* states: "Fighting is unpleasant, and the people of China would prefer not to do it at all. At the same time, they stand ready to wage a just struggle of self-preservation against reactionary elements, both domestic and foreign." When they did it against the United States in the Korean War, the results were disastrous, with an estimated 900,000 troops killed or wounded. Precisely because their record of military success is less than stellar, they tend to be risk averse when it comes to direct conflict.

The modern part is, once again, Qiao and Wang's strong grasp of the power of emerging technologies. You can see this as similar to the invention of gunpowder, but as if there were simultaneously a hundred different kinds of gunpowder.

There are also many new actors beyond just a handful of nations that can make use of that new gunpowder. They foresee a proliferation of terror groups. One they are particularly interested in: Al Qaeda and Osama bin Laden.

They see this as all part of the new world, making clear that their overall philosophy is one of realpolitik, eschewing any need for loyalty or morality.

From Chapter 2 of *Unrestricted Warfare*

... For several thousand years, the three indispensable "hardware" elements of any war have been soldiers, weapons and a battlefield. Running through them all has been the "software" element of warfare: its purposefulness. Before now, nobody has questioned that these are the basic elements of warfare. The problem comes when people discover that all of these basic elements, which seemingly were hard and fast, have changed so that it is impossible to get a firm grip on them. When that day comes, is the war god's face still distinct?

This chapter is getting deeper into the main idea of unrestricted warfare: that the definitions of warriors, weapons, and battlefields have all fundamentally changed, expanding beyond recognition. As the authors note in the next section, this is the first time since Clausewitz that the very purpose of war has been force-fed directly into the bloodstream of a functioning nation-state. Now every civilian is a potential warrior or target, every aspect of modern life is a potential weapon, and every sphere of human activity is a potential battlefield.

Mentioning "the war god's face" is a reference to the literal god of war that all ancient polytheistic cultures prayed to for success. By saying this god's face is indistinct or blurry, the authors are saying that war itself has become disconnected from the weapons and battlefields whence it previously acquired its name. In other words, chivalry and the laws of armed conflict are for suckers. This kind of flowery metaphor is partly why Western strategists and policy makers failed to take *UW* seriously when they first encountered it.

WHY FIGHT AND FOR WHOM?

... As far as their aims, the wars prosecuted by our ancestors were relatively simple in terms of the goals to be achieved. ... This was because our ancestors had limited horizons, their spheres of activity were narrow, they had modest requirements for existence, and their weapons were not lethal enough. ... Just so, Clausewitz wrote his famous saying, which has been an article of faith for several generations of soldiers and statesmen: "War is a continuation of politics." Our ancestors would fight perhaps for the orthodox status of a religious sect, or perhaps for an expanse of pastureland with plenty of water and lush grass. They would not even have scruples about going to war over, say, spices, liquor or a love affair between a king and queen. ... Then there is the war that the English launched against the Qing monarchy for the sake of the opium trade. [Between 1839 and 1860, England and later France enforced their desire to sell opium to the Chinese, inflicting a series of military defeats and leaving an enduring sense of humiliation, which included the lease handover of Hong Kong to the British.] *This was national drug trafficking activity on probably the grandest scale in recorded history. ...*

Prior to recent times, there was just one kind of warfare in terms of the kind of motive and the kind of subsequent actions taken. ...

To assess why people fight is not so easy today, however. In former times, the idea of "exporting revolution" and the slogan of "checking the expansion of communism" were calls to action that elicited countless responses. But especially after the conclusion of the Cold War, when the Iron Curtain running all along the divide between the two great camps [Western Europe and the Soviet Union] *suddenly collapsed, these calls have lost their effectiveness. The times of clearly drawn sides are over.*

Who are our enemies? Who are our friends? These used to be the paramount questions in regard to revolution and counterrevolution. Suddenly the answers have become complicated, confusing and hard to get hold of [because the adversary might be a business partner]. *A country that yesterday was an adversary is in the process of becoming a current partner today, while a country that once was an ally will perhaps be met on the battlefield at the next outbreak of war.... All of this serves to again confirm that old saying: "all friendship is in flux; self-interest is the only constant."...*

The reason for starting a war can be anything from a dispute over territory and resources, a dispute over religious beliefs, hatred stemming from tribal differences or ideology, a dispute over market share, a dispute over the distribution of power and authority, a dispute over trade sanctions, or a dispute stemming from financial unrest. The goals of warfare have become blurred due to the pursuit of a variety of agendas. Thus, it is more and more difficult for people to say clearly just why they are fighting.

Every young lad that participated in the Gulf War will tell you right up front that he fought to restore justice in tiny, weak Kuwait.... In reality, every country that participated in the Gulf War decided to join "Desert Storm" only after carefully thinking over its own intentions and goals. Throughout the whole course of the war, all of the Western powers were fighting for their oil lifeline. To this primary goal, the Americans added the aspiration of building a new world order with "USA" stamped on it. . . . From start to finish, the British reacted enthusiastically to President Bush's [President George H. W. Bush] every move. . . . The French, in order to prevent the complete evaporation of their traditional influence in the Middle East, finally sent troops to the Gulf at the last moment. Naturally, there is no way that a war prosecuted under these kinds of conditions can be a contest fought over a single objective. The aggregate of the self-interests of all the numerous countries participating in the war serves to transform a modern war like "Desert Storm" into a race to further various self-interests under the banner of a common interest. Thus, so-called "common interest" has become merely the war equation's largest common denominator that can be accepted by every allied party participating in the war effort. Since different countries will certainly be pursuing different agendas in a war, it is necessary to take the self-interest of every allied party into consideration if the war is to be prosecuted jointly. . . . The complex interrelationships among self-interests make it impossible to pigeonhole the Gulf War as having been fought for oil, or as having been fought for the new world order, or as having been fought to drive out the invaders. Only a handful of soldiers are likely to grasp a principle that every statesman already knows: that the biggest difference between contemporary wars and the wars of the past is that, in contemporary wars, the overt goal and the covert goal are often two different matters.

In this section the colonels make the accurate point that the purpose of war has expanded dramatically and confusingly beyond traditional conflicts over religion, honor, or land. Note the bitter reference to the Opium Wars of the mid-nineteenth century as an example of old-fashioned war for profit. Because the British humiliated the Chinese, the CCP has consistently used the memory of the Opium Wars to stoke nationalism and hatred of the West. In fact, the Opium Wars are depicted by China's education system and media as the start of the "century of humiliation" from 1849 to 1949 that the CCP is still avenging.

But despite this nod to ancient enmity, the colonels' main point is that allies and enemies are now in constant flux as financial and economic relationships shift. No nation is truly a "friend" to another anymore, if that word was ever valid. Nations don't have friends, only interests. They are warning the CCP not to fall for the language of traditional alliances.

As usual, their favorite example is the Gulf War. They depict the liberation of Kuwait as essentially a fake, PR-driven excuse for the Bush 41 administration to go to war. Defending a helpless, tiny country like Kuwait against the evil forces of Saddam Hussein's Iraq made a great story for the media and inspired the rank-and-file troops, but the colonels claim to see through it. They saw the Gulf War as driven by America's desire to dominate the new world order after the fall of the Soviet Union and to secure a steady supply of Middle Eastern oil. Likewise, they saw Britain and France also driven by oil, as well as by their need to stay in America's good graces. They saw the Western alliance flexing its muscles on the world stage by imposing its will on Iraq while blatantly lying about its motives.

This is obviously an oversimplified and cynical analysis. And we cannot discount the two colonels' biases from their Communist indoctrination. Of course, the United States cared about protecting the West's oil supply, but President Bush's outrage about the invasion of Kuwait also seemed sincere. Countries can and do have multiple goals for a single action, and those goals can blend selfish interests with compassionate altruism. But I would agree that the Chinese don't see it that way.

WHERE TO FIGHT?

... During the long period of time before firearms, battlefields were small and compact. A face-off at close quarters between two armies might unfold on a small expanse of level ground, in a mountain pass, or within the confines of a city. In the eyes of today's soldier, the battlefield that so enraptured the ancients is ... fundamentally incapable of accommodating the spectacle of war as it has unfolded in recent times on such a grand scale....

A soldier's fate is determined by the era in which he lives. [During World War I], *the wingspan of the war god could not extend any farther than the range of a Krupp artillery piece.... 20 years later,* [Hitler] *had long range weapons at his disposal. He utilized bombers powered by Mercedes engines and V-1 and V-2 guided missiles and broke the British Isles' record of never having been encroached upon by an invader. Hitler, who was neither a strategist nor a tactician, ... never really understood the revolutionary significance of breaking through the partition separating battlefield elements from non-battlefield elements....*

This time, technology is again running ahead of the military thinking... [extending] *the contemporary battlefield to a degree that is virtually infinite: there are satellites in space, there are submarines under the water, there are ballistic missiles that can reach anyplace on the globe, and electronic countermeasures are now being carried out in the invisible electromagnetic spectrum space. Even the last refuge of the human race—the inner world of the heart—cannot avoid the attacks of psychological warfare. There are nets above and snares below, so that a person has no place to flee. . . .*

Some extremely imaginative and creative soldiers are just now attempting to introduce these battlespaces into the warfare of the future. The time for a fundamental change in the battlefield—the arena of war—is not far off. Before very long, a network war or a nanometer war might become a reality right in our midst, a type of war that nobody even imagined in the past. It is likely to be very intense, but with practically no bloodshed. Nevertheless, it is likely to determine who is the victor and who the vanquished in an overall war. . . .

The two types of battlespaces—the conventional space and the technological space—will overlap and intersect with each other and will be mutually complementary as each develops in its own way . . . which will all ultimately serve to make up a marvelous battlefield unprecedented in the annals of human warfare. At the same time, with the progressive breaking down of the distinction between military technology and civilian technology, and between the professional soldier and the non-professional warrior, the battlespace will overlap more and more with the non-battlespace, serving also to make the line between these two entities less and less clear. Fields that were formerly isolated from each other are being connected. Mankind is endowing virtually every space with battlefield significance. . . . Just think, if it's even possible to start a war in a computer room or a stock exchange that will send an enemy country to its doom, then is there non-battlespace anywhere?

If that young lad setting out with his orders should ask today: "Where is the battlefield?" The answer would be: "Everywhere."

The new battlespaces that they're describing in this section require close cooperation among a country's military, government, and private sectors. The problem for the United States is that we're still used to seeing those three spheres as quite separate, even as they've become more and more overlapping since the publication of *UW.* Our military strategists, politicians, and business leaders have mostly been locked into the world they grew up with, in which governments set objectives, military forces carried out those objectives, and the private sector's main role was producing material for the military. As the authors put it, technology is changing faster than the ability of strategists to make sense of those changes.

Today's battlefield has no limits, except those we ourselves impose by our own limited perspectives. While physics ultimately restricts what's possible on land, sea, and air, such as the range of a bomber, there are no equivalent limits in cyberspace, other than the creativity of hackers. And in other realms of unrestricted warfare, the limiting factor is how far politicians and business leaders are willing to go.

The last time the United States had true solidarity between the political, military, and private sectors was probably World War II, when everyone who bought war bonds or participated in a scrap metal drive felt like part of the war effort, and when Rosie the Riveters felt like they weren't simply working for a paycheck but were defeating fascism. Today, by contrast, our civilian and business cultures have never been more disconnected and remote from our military culture. Is it even still possible to get them all working toward the same goals, as China does via the top-down control of the CCP?

WHO FIGHTS?

... The era of "strong and brave soldiers who are heroic defenders of the nation" has already passed. In a world where even "nuclear warfare" will perhaps become obsolete military jargon, it is likely that a pasty-faced scholar wearing thick eyeglasses is better suited to be a modern soldier than is a strong young lowbrow with bulging biceps. ...

Modern weapons systems have made it possible for [soldiers] to be far removed from any conventional battlefield, and they can attack the enemy from a place beyond his range of vision where they need not come face to face with the dripping blood that comes with killing. All of this has turned each and every soldier into a self-effacing gentleman who would just as soon avoid the sight of blood. The digital fighter is taking over the role formerly played by the "blood and iron" warrior— a role that, for thousands of years, has not been challenged. ...

Mao Zedong's theory concerning "every citizen a soldier" has certainly not been in any way responsible for this tendency. The current trend does not demand extensive mobilization of the people. Quite the contrary, it merely indicates that a technological elite among the citizenry have broken down the door and barged in uninvited, making it impossible for professional soldiers with their concepts of professionalized warfare to ignore challenges that are somewhat embarrassing.

[This idea of an impertinent technological elite came full circle in 2021, when the CCP leadership cracked down on tech companies and their billionaire entrepreneurs such as Alibaba's Jack Ma. Their wealth and independence had become a threat to the party.]

In 1994, a computer hacker in England attacked the U.S. military's Rome Air Development Center in New York State, compromising the security of 30 systems. He also hacked into more than 100 other systems. . . . What astounded people was not only the scale of those affected by the attack and the magnitude of the damage, but also the fact that the hacker was merely 16 years old. Naturally, an intrusion by a teenager playing a game cannot be regarded as an act of war. The problem is, how does one know for certain which damage is the result of games and which damage is the result of warfare? Which acts are individual acts by citizens and which acts represent hostile actions by non-professional warriors, or perhaps even organized hacker warfare launched by a state? . . .

Whether they are doing good or doing ill, [hackers] *do not feel bound by the rules of the game that prevail in the society at large. . . . They may delete someone else's precious data, that was obtained with such difficulty, as a practical joke. Or, like the legendary lone knight-errant, they may use their outstanding technical skills to take on the evil powers that be. The Suharto government imposed a strict blockade on news about the organized aggressive actions against the ethnic Chinese living in Indonesia. The aggressive actions were first made public on the Internet by witnesses with a sense of justice. As a result, the whole world was utterly shocked, and the Indonesian government and military were pushed before the bar of morality and justice. Prior to this, another group of hackers calling themselves "Milworm" put on another fine performance on the Internet. In order to protest India's nuclear tests, they penetrated the firewall of the network belonging to India's [Bhabha] Atomic Research Center (BARC), altered the home page, and downloaded 5 MB of data. . . .*

The various and sundry monstrous and virtually insane destructive acts by these kinds of groups are undoubtedly more likely to be the new breeding ground for contemporary wars than is the behavior of the lone ranger hacker. Moreover, when a nation state or national armed force (which adheres to certain rules and will only use limited force to obtain a limited goal) faces off with one of these types of organizations (which never observe any rules and which are not afraid to fight an unlimited war using unlimited means), it will often prove very difficult for the nation state or national armed force to gain the upper hand.

More murderous than hackers—and more of a threat in the real world—are the non-state organizations, whose very mention causes the Western world to shake in its boots. These organizations, which all have a certain military flavor to a greater or lesser degree, are generally driven by some extreme creed or cause, such as: the Islamic organizations pursuing a holy war; the Caucasian militias in the U.S.; the Japanese Aum Shinrikyo cult; and, most recently, terrorist groups like Osama bin Ladin's, which blew up the U.S. embassies in Kenya and Tanzania. . . .

During the 1990's [sic], and concurrent with the series of military actions launched by non-professional warriors and non-state organizations, we began to get an inkling of a non-military type of war which is prosecuted by yet another type of non-professional warrior. This person is not a hacker in the general sense of the term, and also is not a member of a quasi-military organization. Perhaps he or she is a systems analyst or a software engineer, or a financier with a large amount of mobile capital, or a stock speculator. He or she might even perhaps be a media mogul who controls a wide variety of media, a famous columnist or the host of a TV program. His or her philosophy of life is different from that of certain blind and inhuman terrorists. Frequently, he or she has a firmly held philosophy of life and his or her faith is by no means inferior to Osama bin Ladin's in terms of its fanaticism. Moreover, he or she does not lack the motivation or courage to enter a fight as necessary. Judging by this kind of standard, who can say that George Soros is not a financial terrorist?

From now on, soldiers no longer have a monopoly on war. Global terrorist activity is one of the by-products of the globalization trend that has been ushered in by technological integration. Non-professional warriors and non-state organizations are posing a greater and greater threat to sovereign nations, making these warriors and organizations more and more serious adversaries for every professional army. Compared to these adversaries, professional armies are like gigantic dinosaurs which lack strength commensurate to their size in this new age. Their adversaries, then, are rodents with great powers of survival, which can use their sharp teeth to torment the better part of the world.

The colonels are drawing an evolutionary time line from traditional warriors to "digital fighters" employed by a military force, to "citizen soldiers" who have no formal ties to the military but can wreak tremendous havoc. They saw the writing on the wall as early as 1994, when that teenage English hacker hinted at far more destructive cyberattacks that would follow, with or without government sponsors. The authors weren't wrong to suggest that autonomous individuals with the right tech skills could approach the power of a nation-state in undermining a dictator like Indonesia's Suharto.

I find it especially interesting that the colonels had Osama bin Laden on their radar as a practitioner of unconventional warfare, more than two years before the attack on the World Trade Center and the Pentagon on September 11, 2001. This made them more prescient than America's intelligence and military establishment, which almost completely missed the potential destructiveness of "non-state organizations" like those nineteen jihadist hijackers armed with nothing more than box cutters.

While we've become much more alert over the past two decades to the threat of terrorism, our military establishment still feels most comfortable planning and training for conventional fighting on conventional battlefields. We're still not prepared for cyberwar attacks like the 2020 breach of multiple agencies and departments of the federal government, presumed to be carried out by Russian hackers. The Pentagon is still focused on getting better and better at fighting conventional wars while our enemies are getting better and better at unconventional attacks that are far more sophisticated than those of 9/11.

And please note that the colonels aren't merely talking about terrorist groups. They are also focused on the financial clout of individuals or companies that can move large amounts of globalized capital in and out of countries for their own gain, which has the potential to wreck economies. They refer to George Soros not as the key figure in current extremist conspiracy theories, but as the currency manipulator whose independent, private sector actions in 1997 triggered a wave of serious financial crises in Southeast Asia. That financial crisis had a profound effect on the CCP leadership and helped spur them to protect their financial system from the West. The authors suggest that the devastation of an intentionally triggered currency crisis can be just as bad as a terrorist attack, even if less literally bloody. And today's financial giants control far more capital that can be weaponized than George Soros did a quarter century ago.

WHAT MEANS AND METHODS ARE USED TO FIGHT?

There's no getting around the opinions of the Americans when it comes to discussing what means and methods will be used to fight future wars. This is not simply because the U.S. is the latest lord of the mountain in the world. It is more because the opinions of the Americans really are superior compared to the prevailing opinions among the military people of other nations. The Americans have summed up the four main forms that warfighting will take in the future as: 1) Information warfare; 2) Precision warfare; 3) Joint operations; and 4) Military operations other than war (MOOTW). This last sentence is a mouthful. From this sentence alone we can see the highly imaginative, and yet highly practical approach of the Americans, and we can also gain a sound understanding of the warfare of the future as seen through the eyes of the Americans. . . .

General Gordon R. Sullivan, the former Chief of Staff of the U.S. Army [1991–95], maintained that information warfare will be the basic form of warfighting in future warfare. For this reason, he set up the best digitized force in the U.S. military, and in the world. Moreover, he proposed the concept of precision warfare, based on the perception that "there will be an overall swing towards information processing and stealthy long-range attacks as the main foundations of future warfare."...

Precision warfare, which has been dubbed "non-contact attack" by the Americans, and "remote combat" by the Russians, is character-ized by concealment, speed, accuracy, a high degree of effectiveness, and few collateral casualties. In wars of the future, where the outcome will perhaps be decided not long after the war starts, this type of tac-tic, which has already showed some of its effectiveness in the Gulf War, will probably be the method of choice that will be embraced most gladly by U.S. generals. However, the phrase that really demonstrates some creative wording is not "information warfare" or "precision war-fare," but rather the phrase "military operations other than war."

[MOOTW] is clearly based on the "world's interest," which the Americans are constantly invoking, and the concept implies a rash overstepping of its authority by the U.S.—a classic case of the Ameri-can attitude that "I am responsible for every place under the sun." Nevertheless, such an assessment does not by any means stifle our praise of this concept, because for the first time it permits a variety of measures that are needed.... Such needed measures include peace-keeping, efforts to suppress illicit drugs, riot suppression, military aid, arms control, disaster relief... and striking at terrorist activities. Contact with this broader concept of war cannot but lessen the sol-diers' attachment to the MOOTW box itself. Ultimately, they will not be able to put the brand-new concept of "non-military war operations" into the box. When this occurs, it will represent an understanding that

*has genuine revolutionary significance in terms of mankind's percep-
tion of war.*

*The difference between the concepts of "non-military war opera-
tions" and "military operations other than war" is far greater than a
surface reading would indicate and is by no means simply a matter
of changing the order of some words in a kind of word game. The latter
concept, MOOTW, may be considered simply an explicit label for missions and operations by armed forces that are carried out when there
is no state of war. The former concept, "non-military war operations,"
extends our understanding of exactly what constitutes a state of war
to each and every field of human endeavor, far beyond what can be
embraced by the term "military operations." This type of extension is
the natural result of the fact that human beings will use every conceivable means to achieve their goals. While it seems that the Americans
are in the lead in every field of military theory, they were not able to
take the lead in proposing this new concept of war. However, we cannot fail to recognize that the flood of U.S.-style pragmatism around
the world, and the unlimited possibilities offered by new, high technology, were nevertheless powerful forces behind the emergence of
this concept.*

While there has been much praise over the years for the precision capabilities of the American military, Qiao and Wang make
clear that they are talking about something completely different.
Interestingly, they find this less lethal form of war to be admirable—
in a rare compliment to the United States. But they still see it resid-
ing in a traditional sphere of military control and doctrine. We're
playing checkers and they're playing 3D chess.

Of the four types of future warfare addressed in this section, three evolved from existing military traditions. The Western military strategists we discussed in previous chapters, like Boyd and Warden, would appreciate today's level of precision warfare and the Pentagon's focus on speed and lethality on the battlefield. They would recognize the increasing focus on joint operations—the effort to get the different service branches working together more cohesively—which played such a huge role during our post–9/11 invasions and occupations of Afghanistan and Iraq. They'd also understand today's information warfare as the evolution of traditional propaganda, now done via social media and email blasts rather than leaflet drops from the air or unauthorized radio broadcasts into an enemy's frequencies.

But they might have a harder time wrapping their minds around military operations other than war, which can be defined as using a military force to deter war, resolve conflicts, promote peace, and support civil authorities in response to domestic crises. This concept goes against the traditional definition of military force, but it has played an increasingly large role in Pentagon thinking over the past two decades. In Iraq and Afghanistan, MOOTW included the controversial adoption of counterinsurgency (COIN) as a top priority by occupation forces to win over civilian populations that were being recruited by jihadist terrorist groups.

The effectiveness of COIN and other MOOTW initiatives during those occupations are still being debated, but what matters for this discussion is how hard it was for most of our senior military leadership to adapt to this new paradigm. Many resisted the idea that highly trained warriors would need to focus on winning civilian hearts and minds more than on blowing up military targets and killing our enemies before they could kill us. And yet this conception of MOOTW was much less radical than the brand of unrestricted warfare that the CCP was practicing by the early 2000s. Because of *UW,* China got a huge head start on information warfare, as well as the many other forms of nonmilitary operations introduced in the rest of this chapter. And the CCP saw America's arrogance preventing us from understanding what China was doing while we were distracted by long and frustrating engagements in the Middle East.

NONMILITARY WAR OPERATIONS: TRADE WAR AND FINANCIAL WAR

So, which [of many kinds of unconventional] means, which seem totally unrelated to war, will ultimately become the favored minions of this new type of war—"the non-military war operation"—being waged with greater and greater frequency all around the world?

    Trade War: About a dozen years ago, "trade war" was still simply a descriptive phrase, but today it has become a tool in the hands of many countries for waging non-military warfare. It can be used with particularly great skill in the hands of the Americans, who have perfected it to a fine art. Some of the means used include: the use of domestic trade law on the international stage; the arbitrary erection and dismantling of tariff barriers; the use of hastily written trade sanctions; the imposition of embargoes on exports of critical technologies; the use of the Special Section 301 law; and the application of most-favored-nation (MFN) treatment, etc., etc. Any one of these means

can have a destructive effect that is equal to that of a military opera-
tion. The comprehensive eight-year embargo against Iraq that was initi-
ated by the U.S. is the most classic textbook example in this regard.

Financial War: Now that Asians have experienced the financial
crisis in Southeast Asia, no one could be more affected by "financial
war" than they have been.... A surprise financial war attack that was
deliberately planned and initiated by the owners of international mo-
bile capital ultimately served to pin one nation after another to the
ground—nations that not long ago were hailed as "little tigers" and
"little dragons." [Those phrases refer to South Korea, Taiwan, Hong
Kong, and Singapore.] *Economic prosperity that once excited the*
constant admiration of the Western world changed to a depression,
like the leaves of a tree that are blown away in a single night by the
autumn wind. After just one round of fighting, the economies of a
number of countries had fallen back ten years. What is more, such a
defeat on the economic front precipitates a near collapse of the social
and political order. The casualties resulting from the constant chaos
are no less than those resulting from a regional war, and the injury
done to the living social organism even exceeds the injury inflicted by
a regional war....

Thus, financial war is a form of non-military warfare which is just
as terribly destructive as a bloody war, but in which no blood is actu-
ally shed.... We believe that before long, "financial warfare" will un-
doubtedly be an entry in the various types of dictionaries of official
military jargon. Moreover, when people revise the history books on
[late-] *twentieth-century warfare, the section on financial warfare*
will command the reader's utmost attention. The main protagonist
will not be a statesman or a military strategist; rather, it will be George

Soros. . . . After Soros began his activities, Li Denghui [Taiwan's president from 1988 to 2000] *used the financial crisis in Southeast Asia to
devalue the New Taiwan dollar, so as to launch an attack on the Hong
Kong dollar and Hong Kong stocks. . . .*

*In addition, . . . large and small speculators have come en masse
to this huge dinner party for money gluttons, including Morgan Stanley and Moody's, which are famous for the credit rating reports that
they issue, and which point out promising targets of attack for the
benefit of the big fish in the financial world. These two companies are
typical of those entities that participate indirectly in the great feast
and reap the benefits.*

*In the summer of 1998, after the fighting in the financial war had
been going on for a full year, the war's second round of battles began
to unfold on an even more extensive battlefield, and this round of
battles continues to this day. This time, it was not just the countries of
Southeast Asia (which had suffered such a crushing defeat during the
previous year) that were drawn into the war. Two titans were also
drawn in—Japan and Russia. This resulted in making the global economic situation even more grim and difficult to control. . . .*

*Today, when nuclear weapons have already become frighten-
ing mantlepiece decorations that are losing their real operational
value with each passing day, financial war has become a "hyperstra-
tegic" weapon that is attracting the attention of the world. This is
because financial war is easily manipulated, allows for concealed
actions, and is also highly destructive. . . . Perhaps we could dub this
type of war "foundation-style" financial war. The greater and greater
frequency and intensity of this type of war, and the fact that more
and more countries and non-state organizations are deliberately*

using it, are causes for concern and are facts that we must face squarely.

Trade war and financial war aren't metaphors to the authors of *UW*—they are seen as very real forms of war. The colonels see the U.S. Congress's annual vote against China's Most Favored Nation trade status as an act of war against the Chinese, as are the International Monetary Fund's tight monetary policies and China's exclusion from the World Trade Organization, which lasted until December 2001. These kinds of grievances stoke the CCP's ongoing resentment of and belligerence toward the West. In particular, the Asian financial crisis of 1997 made a huge impression on them. Capital flight from Asia and the new requirements of the IMF showed the CCP how much unilateral power the United States had in the global financial system. Secure access to capital became an extremely critical issue.

Section 301 refers to part of the U.S. Trade Act of 1974, which authorizes the president to take all appropriate action, including tariff-based retaliation, to respond to any foreign government that violates an international trade agreement or acts in an unjustified or unreasonable way on trade, especially regarding alleged violations of intellectual property. It's another aspect of our economic relationship that made the CCP feel like the United States was the aggressor against China, not the reverse.

For America's political and military establishment, however, financial and trade policies have nothing to do with warfare. I doubt anyone in the Pentagon was even paying attention to the headlines about capital flight and currency manipulation in 1997. The Clinton administration saw the Asian financial crisis as a multilateral issue that had to be handled mainly by global organizations like the IMF. And they certainly took no responsibility for private sector financial players like George Soros or Morgan Stanley. They saw the financial crisis as an unfortunate consequence of globalized financial markets, not an act of aggression by the United States against the Asian countries. Likewise, I had never even heard of Section 301 during my career as an Air Force officer until I got to the White House in 2017.

In response to the Asian financial crisis, the CCP did more to insulate their economy from outside attacks. Today they have a nonconvertible currency and strict capital controls. They are even moving forward with a digital currency that won't be subject to the global financial markets—a Chinese version of bitcoin.

The authors are right that financial war can be especially devastating because it can be planned and executed stealthily, often concealed via proxies in the private sector. The CCP uses its insulated banking system, Chinese companies, and other nongovernmental organizations as its proxies in ongoing financial warfare. They didn't invent these tactics, but they've adapted them from malicious individuals and terrorist groups, as we'll see in the chapters ahead.

NONMILITARY WAR OPERATIONS: TERROR WAR AND ECOLOGICAL WAR

New Terror War in Contrast to Traditional Terror War: Due to the limited scale of a traditional terror war, its casualties might well be fewer than the casualties resulting from a conventional war or campaign. Nevertheless, a traditional terror war carries a stronger flavor of violence . . . [because] *it is never bound by any of the traditional rules of the society at large. From a military standpoint, then, the traditional terror war is characterized by the use of limited resources to fight an unlimited war. This characteristic invariably puts national forces in an extremely unfavorable position even before war breaks out, since national forces must always conduct themselves according to certain rules and therefore are only able to use their unlimited resources to fight a limited war. This explains how a terrorist organization made up of just a few inexperienced members who are still wet behind the ears can nevertheless give a mighty country like the U.S. headaches, and also why "using a sledgehammer to kill an ant" often proves ineffective. The most recent proof is the case of the two explosions that occurred simultaneously at the U.S. embassies in Nairobi and Dar es Salaam. The advent of bin Ladin–style terrorism has deepened the impression that a national force, no matter how powerful, will find it difficult to gain the upper hand in a game that has no rules. Even if a country turns itself into a terrorist element, as the Americans are now in the process of doing, it will not necessarily be able to achieve success.*

Be that as it may, if all terrorists confined their operations simply to the traditional approach of bombings, kidnappings, assassinations, and plane hijackings, this would represent less than the maximum degree of terror. What really strikes terror into people's hearts is the rendezvous of terrorists with various types of new, high technologies that possibly will evolve into new superweapons. We already have a hint of what the future may hold. . . . When Aum Shinrikyo followers discharged "Sarin" poison gas in a Tokyo subway, the casualties re-

sulting from the poison gas accounted for just a small portion of the terror. This affair put people on notice that modern biochemical technology had already forged a lethal weapon for those terrorists who would try to carry out the mass destruction of humanity. . . . [Other terrorist groups] *specialize in breaking into the computer networks of banks and news organizations, stealing stored data, deleting programs, and disseminating disinformation. . . . This type of terrorist operation uses the latest technology in the most current fields of study, and sets itself against humanity as a whole. We might well call this type of operation "new terror war."*

Ecological War: This refers to a new type of non-military warfare in which modern technology is employed to influence the natural state of rivers, oceans, the crust of the earth, the polar ice sheets, the air circulating in the atmosphere, and the ozone layer. By methods such as causing earthquakes and altering precipitation patterns, the atmospheric temperature, the composition of the atmosphere, sea level height, and sunshine patterns, the earth's physical environment is damaged, or an alternate local ecology is created. Perhaps before very long, a man-made El Nino or La Nina effect will become yet another kind of superweapon in the hands of certain nations and/or non-state organizations. It is more likely that a non-state organization will become the prime initiator of ecological war, because of its terrorist nature, because it feels it has no responsibility to the people or to the society at large, and because non-state organizations have consistently demonstrated that they [are] *unwilling to play by the rules of the game. Moreover, since the global ecological environment will frequently be on the borderline of catastrophe as nations strive for the most rapid development possible, there is a real danger that the slightest increase or decrease in any variable would be enough to touch off an ecological holocaust.*

Again, I have to note how savvy the colonels were about terrorism and their reference to Osama bin Laden, more than two years before 9/11. They understood that traditional militaries—including the world's sole remaining superpower—were unprepared for a fight against terrorists willing to ignore international laws and norms of combat. They saw that the politics and bureaucracy of the United States would make it very hard to identify and stop terrorists who engaged in unrestricted warfare. The metaphor of "using a sledgehammer to kill an ant" is a depressing but not inaccurate way to describe the Bush administration's War on Terror.

The authors also understood that a successful plane hijacking or biochemical attack would have repercussions far beyond the actual number of casualties, as could cyberattacks that wipe out bank accounts or disrupt electrical grids. It's not that they were suggesting these specific tactics to the CCP, but they were taking an inventory of all the possible options for unconventional warfare. This ruthless inventory of options must concern our national security types, especially after the extended crisis caused by the coronavirus—or are we too fixated to recognize the kind of opportunities the CCP would eagerly exploit?

The next part, about ecological warfare, sounded crazy to me when I first encountered *UW.* Yet twenty years later, we have a much clearer picture of the long-term threat of climate change and China's role in making it worse. The CCP leads the world in emissions of carbon dioxide, which is heating up the planet at increasing speed.* China is also the worst offender in overfishing the oceans in its never-ending quest to feed its massive population.† As with every other subject the CCP comments on, we can't believe a word about China's intent to fight climate change, despite its signing of the Paris Agreement. For instance, China has been going full speed ahead on fracking.‡

Nevertheless, climate activists like Greta Thunberg never seem to criticize China for its role in widespread ecological devastation over the past two decades. Instead, they tend to focus on the sins of the West and often fall for misinformation about China's efforts to go green. These misinformation campaigns, launched by the CCP and amplified by climate activists and international organizations like the UN, are an example of information warfare intersecting with ecological warfare. The UN also looks the other way in part because of the CCP's widespread graft and influence efforts against its bureaucrats.

Meanwhile, Americans accept damaging restrictions to their economy for the sake of climate change, accelerating widespread job losses as "dirty" manufacturing jobs continue to move offshore— often to China, where companies can pollute with little or no restriction. And American politicians want to ban fracking, even

---

*Andriy Blokhin, "The 5 Countries That Produce the Most Carbon Dioxide (CO2)," Investopedia, August 28, 2021, https://www.investopedia.com/articles/investing/092915/5-countries-produce-most-carbon-dioxide-co2.asp.

†Matthew Carney, "China's Super Trawlers Are Stripping the Ocean Bare as Its Hunger for Seafood Grows," ABC News, September 29, 2018, updated October 4, 2018, https://www.abc.net.au/news/2018-09-30/china-super-trawlers-overfishing-world-oceans/10317394.

‡Steven Lee Myers, "China Experiences a Fracking Boom, and All the Problems That Go with It," *New York Times*, March 8, 2019, https://www.nytimes.com/2019/03/08/world/asia/china-shale-gas-fracking.html.

though the dangers of the process are exaggerated and it has helped drive our cost of natural gas to the lowest in the world.*

I'm not sure that a man-made El Niño climate effect is likely, but China's use of climate change as yet another opportunity to deceive and manipulate the West is deeply disturbing.

MORE TYPES OF NONMILITARY WARFARE

Aside from what we have discussed above, we can point out a number of other means and methods used to fight a non-military war, some of which already exist and some of which may exist in the future. Such means and methods include:

- *Psychological warfare (spreading rumors to intimidate the enemy and break his will)*
- *Smuggling warfare (throwing markets into confusion and attacking economic order)*
- *Media warfare (manipulating what people see and hear in order to lead public opinion)*
- *Drug warfare (obtaining sudden and huge illicit profits by spreading disaster in other countries)*
- *Network warfare (venturing out in secret and concealing one's identity in a type of warfare that is virtually impossible to guard against)*

---

*Christopher M. Matthews, "What Would Happen If the U.S. Banned Fracking?," *Wall Street Journal*, November 19, 2019, https://www.wsj.com/articles/what-would-happen-if-the-u-s-banned-fracking-11574208146.

- *Technological warfare (creating monopolies by setting standards independently)*
- *Fabrication warfare (presenting a counterfeit appearance of real strength before the eyes of the enemy)*
- *Resources warfare (grabbing riches by plundering stores of resources)*
- *Economic aid warfare (bestowing favor in the open and contriving to control matters in secret)*
- *Cultural warfare (leading cultural trends along in order to assimilate those with different views)*
- *International law warfare (seizing the earliest opportunity to set up regulations)*

In addition, there are other types of non-military warfare which are too numerous to mention. In this age, when the plethora of new technologies can in turn give rise to a plethora of new means and methods of fighting war, (not to mention the cross-combining and creative use of these means and methods), it would simply be senseless and a waste of effort to list all of the means and methods one by one.... Faced with a nearly infinitely diverse array of options to choose from, why do people want to enmesh themselves in a web of their own making and select and use means of warfare that are limited to the realm of the force of arms and military power? Methods that are not characterized by the use of the force of arms, nor by the use of military power, nor even by the presence of casualties and bloodshed, are just as likely to facilitate the successful realization of the war's goals, if not more so.... This prospect has led to revision of the statement that "war is politics with bloodshed," and in turn has also led to a change in the hitherto set view that warfare through force of arms is the ultimate means of resolving conflict. . . .

The enlargement of the concept of warfare has, in turn, resulted in enlargement of the realm of war-related activities. . . . Any war that breaks out tomorrow or further down the road will be characterized by warfare in the broad sense—a cocktail mixture of warfare prosecuted through the force of arms and warfare prosecuted by means other than the force of arms.

The goal of this kind of warfare will encompass more than merely "using means that involve the force of arms to force the enemy to accept one's own will." Rather, the goal should be "to use all means whatsoever—means that involve military power and means that do not involve military power, means that entail casualties and means that do not entail casualties—to force the enemy to serve one's own interests."

This section concludes the chapter by showing how creative the colonels were in their vision of unrestricted warfare. The CCP has used virtually all of their nonmilitary tactics at one time or another, even the ones you've probably never heard of.

Smuggling warfare? Chinese transshipments—the practice of moving cargo to a third party country to evade tariffs or other regulations—are undermining U.S. trade policies that aim to prevent China from dumping cheap products on our markets.*

Media warfare? The CCP has pursued an aggressive campaign to influence Hollywood's depictions of China. "China is the number

---

*Patrick Conway, "How Transshipment May Undercut Trump's Tariffs," *The Conversation*, April 26, 2018, https://theconversation.com/how-transshipment-may-undercut-trumps-tariffs-95487.

two biggest movie-going country in the world. So, it's only natural for American movie makers to try to please the cultural gate-keepers of the Chinese government. They've been doing it for years."*

Drug warfare? The CCP has smuggled fentanyl, among other drugs, into the United States. "U.S. Immigration and Customs Enforcement has identified China as the primary source of illicit fentanyl and the painkiller's analogues that enter our country. Drug traffickers use two primary techniques for delivering fentanyl manufactured in China: It is either shipped directly into the U.S. via international mail or shipped into Mexico to be smuggled into America."†

Network warfare? The Justice Department has charged China with cyberattacks against more than one hundred American companies. "The Department of Justice has used every tool available to disrupt the illegal computer intrusions and cyberattacks by these Chinese citizens," then Deputy Attorney General Jeffrey Rosen told *The Wall Street Journal* in September 2020. "Regrettably, the Chinese Communist Party has chosen a different path of making China safe for cybercriminals so long as they attack computers outside China and steal intellectual property helpful to China."‡

---

*Stephen Colbert, "How China Is Taking Control of Hollywood," interview by Tim Doescher, *Heritage Explains,* The Heritage Foundation, December 13, 2018, https://www.heritage .org/asia/heritage-explains/how-china-taking-control-hollywood.

†Hans A. von Spakovsky and Peyton Smith, "China Is Poisoning America with Fentanyl," The Heritage Foundation, March 5, 2019, https://www.heritage.org/crime-and-justice /commentary/china-poisoning-america-fentanyl.

‡Dustin Volz, Aruna Viswanatha, and Kate O'Keeffe, "U.S. Charges Chinese Nationals in Cyberattacks on More Than 100 Companies," *Wall Street Journal,* September 16, 2020, https://www.wsj.com/articles/justice-department-unseals-indictments-alleging -chinese-hacking-against-u-s-international-firms-11600269024.

Tech warfare? China is trying to dominate international standards for the 5G wireless networks. "The US-China competition is essentially about who will control the global information technology infrastructure and standards," said Frank Rose, a military analyst and former assistant secretary of state for arms control, in May 2020. "I think an argument can be made that in the 21st century, whoever controls the information infrastructure will dominate the world."*

Resources warfare? China has been trying to dominate the market for increasingly essential rare earth metals. According to *The Detroit News* in November 2020, "China now supplies 80% of the rare earth metals used in the United States, partly because it follows lower environmental protection standards than the United States and other advanced countries. Beijing is also expanding its stunning lead in the lithium-ion battery industry. China has increased the number of planned battery mega-factories to 107, with 53 now active and in production. In contrast, the U.S. has only nine battery mega-factories in the pipeline. The future of America's auto industry—and the millions of jobs it supports—hangs in the balance."†

Economic aid warfare? That's an accurate term for China's Belt and Road Initiative, designed to "forge closer ties, deepen cooperation and expand the development space in the Eurasian region." In

---

*Theresa Hitchens, "US Risks Losing 5G Standard Setting Battle to China, Experts Say," *Breaking Defense*, May 11, 2020, https://breakingdefense.com/2020/05/us-risks-losing-5g-standard-setting-battle-to-china-experts-say.

†John Adams, "Opinion: China Controls Rare Minerals America Needs for the Future," *Detroit News*, November 8, 2020, https://www.detroitnews.com/story/opinion/2020/11/09/opinion-china-controls-rare-minerals-america-needs-future/6174603002.

other words, it's a way to lock in the loyalty of countries in that region through seemingly generous economic aid.*

International law warfare? According to The Heritage Foundation, "Legal warfare is one of the key instruments of psychological and public opinion/media warfare. It raises doubts among adversary and neutral military and civilian authorities, as well as the broader population, about the legality of adversary actions, thereby diminishing political will and support—and potentially retarding military activity. It also provides material for public opinion/media warfare."†

As we saw in the introduction with COVID-19, China has gotten good at combining these and other tactics for maximum impact, including media warfare, disinformation, and a reckless disregard for the health and safety of innocent civilians around the world.

When I first encountered *UW* two decades ago, I couldn't believe that these PLA colonels were describing all these kinds of "war" in a literal rather than a metaphoric sense. Like the Pentagon's top brass, I failed to take this kind of language seriously while I focused on getting better and better at conventional warfare. But these kinds of war are as serious and as deadly as any of us can imagine. Every day that we fail to prepare for these unconventional attacks is another day that slowly erodes the vitality of our nation.

---

*Nadège Rolland, "A Concise Guide to the Belt and Road Initiative," National Bureau of Asian Research, April 11, 2019, https://www.nbr.org/publication/a-guide-to-the-belt-and-road-initiative.

†Dean Cheng, "Winning Without Fighting: Chinese Legal Warfare," The Heritage Foundation, May 21, 2012, https://www.heritage.org/asia/report/winning-without-fighting-chinese-legal-warfare.

CHAPTER 6

DESERT STORM:
A MILITARY MASTERPIECE

THE COLONELS' CASE STUDY OF THE FIRST GULF WAR IS ES-
sential to understanding their thinking. It was much studied at
many levels of the Chinese government and military throughout
the 1990s. But it was Qiao and Wang who drew out a complex series
of lessons that we see reflected in Beijing's strategic thinking to
this date.

In the view of the colonels, Operation Desert Storm was something of a pyrrhic victory. Brilliant win. Wrong lessons. This chapter is the most insightful analysis of that war that I've ever seen.
Qiao and Wang understand the after-action analysis of that war—
for good and bad—better than our own military analysts. They
take a deep and sophisticated dive into the factors that underlay
the U.S. success, displaying a thorough understanding of things
like the U.S. command structure and how recent reforms stream-
lined decision-making. They have done their homework.

They admire the diplomatic foundation that helped establish both
the legitimacy of the war and the broad coalition of countries that

helped the United States. China learned the value of infiltrating inter-national organizations. Similarly, the large role of the media, especially twenty-four-hour global cable television, in shaping the war has led to the CCP's obsession with controlling its own media and shutting out the rest of the world. As the colonels write, *We might as well say that, intentionally or otherwise, the U.S. military and the Western media joined hands to form a noose to hang Saddam's Iraq from the gallows.*

But they argue that the rapid victory based on many tech weap-ons built an assumption that all future wars would be so easy.

It's important to remember that while *Unrestricted War* in-cludes many new definitions of war, it does not exclude the old forms of war: The colonels' point is not either/or; it is "all of the above." This dissection of a kinetic war may be most useful as we start to think about Taiwan and the increasingly strident rhetoric about reunification coming from Xi Jinping and his comrades.

Everything the colonels write would suggest a full-scale mili-tary invasion is the last thing the Chinese want—yet might be the last thing they do. But in the meantime, we should expect an end-less series of feints and provocations, propaganda campaigns, po-litical and financial coercions. We need a carefully crafted policy to understand and blunt those aggressions.

From Chapter 3 of *Unrestricted Warfare*

A CLASSIC WAR

Perhaps because victory [in the Gulf War] *was achieved so easily, to this day there are very few people in Uncle Sam's wildly jubilant group that have accurately evaluated the significance of the war. Some hot-heads used this to ceaselessly fabricate the myth that the United States was invincible, while some who could still be considered cool-headed—most of whom were commentators and generals unable to take part in "Desert Storm" in a complex and subtle frame of mind—believed that "Desert Storm" was not a typical war, and that a war conducted under such ideal conditions cannot serve as a model. . . . We have no intention of helping the Americans create a myth, but when "Desert Storm" unfolded and concluded for all to see, with its many combatant countries, enormous scale, short duration, small number of casualties, and glorious results startling the whole world, who could say that a classic war heralding the arrival of warfare in the age of technical integration-globalization had not opened wide the main front door to the mysterious and strange history of warfare. . . .*

When we attempt to use wars that have already occurred to discuss what constitutes war in the age of technical integration-globalization, only "Desert Storm" can provide ready-made examples. At present, in any sense it is still not just the only [example], but the classic [example], and therefore it is the only "apple" that is worthy of our close analysis. . . .

The colonels start by correctly noting the many noteworthy elements—military, diplomatic, technological, and media driven—that came together in a unique way. In some respects, Desert Storm was a harbinger of future international conflicts, including the use of unrestricted warfare. But in other ways it was a unique moment in history that will never come close to being repeated. The authors call it "an apple with numerous sections" that can be studied only by pulling the sections apart.

It's also a "classic war" because it applied cutting-edge technology to classic Western military strategy. The success of America's superior technology against the well-equipped Iraqi forces—including the amazing power of our satellite-guided navigation systems and precision laser-guided weapons delivered from stealth aircraft—renewed American interest in the theory of the Revolution in Military Affairs in the 1990s and 2000s. RMA suggested that we should focus our efforts and resources on maintaining and extending our technological superiority as the key to a strong national defense. Unfortunately, RMA proved to be the completely wrong response to the soon-to-emerge Chinese strategy of unrestricted warfare. Nonetheless, this idea of using Silicon Valley to make killing more efficient continues to prevail.

THE "OVERNIGHT" ALLIANCE

From Saddam's perspective, annexing Kuwait seemed more like a household matter in the extended Arab family compared to the taking of American hostages during the Iranian revolution, and besides, he had given notice ahead of time. However, he overlooked the differences between the two. When Iran took the hostages, it was certainly a slap in the Americans' face, but Iraq had seized the entire West by the throat. Lifelines are naturally more important than face, and the United States had no choice but to take it seriously, while other countries which felt threatened by Iraq also had to take it seriously. In their alliance with the United States, what most of the Arab countries had in mind was rooting out the Islamic heresy represented by Saddam to keep him from damaging their own interests were he to grow stronger unopposed, and it is very difficult to really say that they wanted to extend justice to Kuwait.

The common concerns about their interests enabled the United States to weave an allied network to catch Iraq very quickly. . . . Numerous countries volunteered to be responsible nodes in this alliance network. Although they were unwilling, Germany and Japan finally seemed actually happy to open their purses, and what was more important than providing money was that neither of them lost the opportunity to send their own military personnel, thereby taking a stealthy and symbolic step toward again becoming global powers. Egypt persuaded Libya and Jordan to be neutral in the war and no longer support Iraq, so that Saddam became thoroughly isolated. Even Gorbachev, who wanted to get the Americans' support for his weak position domestically, ultimately tacitly recognized the military strikes of the multinational forces against his old ally.

Even powers such as the United States must similarly rely on the support of its allies, and this support was primarily manifested in providing legitimacy for its actions and in logistical support, not in adding so many troops. The reason that President Bush's policies were able to get widespread approval from the American public was to a great extent due to the fact that he had established an international alliance, thereby getting the people to believe that this was not a case of pulling someone else's chestnuts out of the fire, and it was not just the Americans who were funding the war and preparing to have their blood spilled. They went so far as to send the VII Corps from Germany to Saudi Arabia, mobilizing 465 trains, 312 barges, and 119 fleets from four NATO countries. At the same time, Japan also provided the electronics parts urgently needed by U.S. military equipment, and this further demonstrated the increasing reliance of the United States on its allies. In the new age, "going it alone" is not only unwise, it is also not a realistic option. . . . From the Security Council's Resolution 660 calling for Iraq to withdraw from Kuwait to Resolution 678 which authorized the member countries to take any actions, international society broadly identified itself with the alliance which was temporarily cobbled together. One hundred and ten countries took part in the embargo against Iraq, and more than 30 countries took part in the use of force, including numerous Arab countries! Obviously, every country had fully estimated where its interests were prior to this action.

The full-scale intervention of the United Nations was not sufficient to make it possible for this fragile and spider-web like alliance, which was formed in a very short period of time, to easily withstand the impact of a war. It can be said that, as far as the politicians were concerned, the alliance was only a single high-level meeting following a careful weighing of interests, a single contract signing, or even a verbal promise via a hot-line. However, for the troops carrying out the allied warfare, no detail could be overlooked. To avoid having U.S. soldiers violate Muslim commandments, in addition to stipulating that they must abide strictly by the customs of the country in which they were stationed, the U.S. military even leased a "Cunard Princess" yacht and anchored it at sea to provide Western-style amusements for the U.S troops. To prevent the Israelis from retaliating against the "Scud" missile attacks and throwing the camp which was assaulting Iraq into disorder, the United States made a tremendous effort to provide the Israelis with air support, taking great pains to look after the alliance network.

More profoundly, the appearance of the "overnight" alliance brought an era to a close. That is, the age of fixed-form alliances which had begun with the signing of the military alliance between Germany and Austria-Hungary in 1879. Following the Cold War, the period in which alliances were formed on the basis of ideology faded away, while the approach in which alliances are built on interests rose to primacy. Under the general banner of realpolitik, in which national interests are paramount, any alliance can only be focused more nakedly on interests, and at times they don't even feel like raising the banner of morality. Without a doubt, the alliance phenomenon will continue to exist, but in more cases they will be loose and short-term interest coalitions.

Which is also to say that there will no longer be any alliances where only morality, not interests, are involved. Different periods have different interests and goals, and that will be what determines whether there are alliances or not. Increasingly pragmatic and unconstrained by any moral fetters, this is the characteristic feature of modern alliances. All forces are united by a network of interests, and they may be very short-lived but extremely effective. The interest relationships of modern states, as well as among trans-national organizations and even among regional forces have thus begun to be increasingly transitory. . . . Today's mode of ever-changing combinations of force, along with the age of ever-changing technological integration and globalization, has given rise to certain tacit alliances which are by no means fortuitous. Therefore, the "overnight" alliance that was formed by the Gulf War formally opened the curtain to a new alliance era.

This section makes the excellent point that the anti-Iraq alliance that fought in the Gulf War was unlike any other in modern history. It's important to understand how it differed from alliances of the preceding half century, the Cold War era.

The United States was forced to stand up to Iraq because its seizure of Kuwait's oil fields was an unacceptable threat to our energy supply—it "seized the entire West by the throat." As they've said previously, the colonels believe that oil was the only reason for the war, but I believe President Bush was also genuinely outraged by Iraq's brazen occupation of Kuwait. Both can be true at the same time. Likewise, our allies in Desert Storm had a wide range of incentives to be part of the coalition, some of them as self-interested as a desire to stay in the good graces of the United States.

The part that's most prescient is their prediction that ad hoc, short-term alliances would replace long-term alliances such as NATO and the Warsaw Pact. With the end of the Cold War, there was no more need for an entrenched global coalition against an ideological foe like the Soviet Union. The colonels were right that future coalitions would follow the model of Desert Storm. After a new crisis erupts, various nations come together to address it, with or without the influence of the United Nations or other global organizations. Then the allies go their separate ways again. We saw this new model continue after 9/11, in Afghanistan and the Iraq War.

The authors also correctly depicted the UN as an organizing entity for solidifying international support for a state's chosen policy options. This insight subsequently led to the CCP's widespread infiltration of institutions within the UN as well as other world organizations. These infiltrations paid off very effectively in 2020, when the Western democratic countries mostly believed the false coronavirus information that China disseminated via the UN and the World Health Organization. As I wrote earlier, the CCP's manipulation of the coronavirus pandemic is probably the most striking example to date of its successful use of unrestricted warfare.

TIMELY "REORGANIZATION ACT"

... U.S. aircraft which bombed Vietnam 30 years ago had to listen to commands from four different headquarters at the same time.... Up until about 15 years ago, there were separate and independent command systems, and it was not clear who was in authority, and this had disastrous consequences for U.S. troops stationed in Beirut, as it led directly to approximately 200 Marines losing their lives.... [During the Lebanese civil war in October 1983, the U.S. Marine barracks in Beirut, Lebanon, were struck by a truck bomb that killed 241 service members, including 220 Marines.] *Even after he was made commander-in-chief of the allied forces during "Desert Storm," the problem that was exposed in Grenada was still fresh in the memory of General Norman Schwarzkopf. When he was deputy commander of the joint task force during the "Grenada" action, each of the service arms of the U.S. forces taking part in the action went its own way. The question ... was, during joint operations, just who listens to whose commands?*

It is somewhat ironic that this problem, which had troubled the U.S. military for several decades, was not overcome by generals who had experienced extensive combat, or experts who were steeped in statecraft, but by two congressmen named Goldwater and Nichols [Sen. Barry Goldwater and Rep. Bill Nichols]. *The "DOD Reorganization*

Act" proposed by these two which was passed by Congress in 1986, used the legislative approach to resolve the problem of unified command of the various armed services during joint combat. . . .

[Colin] Powell and Schwarzkopf were the lucky earliest beneficiaries of the "Reorganization Act" and at the same time they also became the two most powerful generals in the history of American warfare. As the Chairman of the Joint Chiefs of Staff (JCS), Powell for the first time had clearly attained the position of the President's chief military adviser, which enabled him to take orders directly from the President and the Secretary of Defense, as well as issue orders to the three services based on that; and he no longer had to serve as the coordinator for the endless wrangling that took place among the chiefs of staff of the armed services. As the battlefield commander, Schwarzkopf was spared the nagging and held the real power in his hands. As for the incessant chatter coming from the Pentagon, he was free to choose what to listen to and to do what he wanted. . . . This made it possible for him to exercise the trans-service authority granted to the commander of the joint headquarters by the "DOD Reorganization Act" without any hesitation when necessary. . . .

That a law which had not been in effect for five years could be implemented so thoroughly in a war that came along at the same time must be attributed to the contractual mentality of the people in the legal society represented by the United States. Furthermore, the new pattern of command which was derived from this became the most successful and fitting application of military command since the services were divided. Its direct result was to reduce the levels of command, implementing true entrusted command and causing the old, deeply-rooted tree-structure command system to start to evolve to-

ward a network structure; and a side effect of this evolution was to enable more combat units to share first-time battlefield information.

If the "Reorganization Act" is considered against the wider backdrop of the age, it is not difficult to discover that this reorganization of the U.S. military was by no means a chance coincidence, but was timely and in conformity with the natural demands the new age posed for the old military command relations, that is, by recombining the service arm authority that was originally dispersed, then on that basis generating a super-authority that overrode the authority of all the service arms and which was concentrated on certain temporary goals, it became possible to be more than equal to the task in any battlefield contest. The emergence of the "Reorganization Act" in the United States and the effects it produced in the U.S. military are food for thought, and any country which hopes to win a war in the 21st century must inevitably face the option of either "reorganizing" or being defeated. There is no other way.

The colonels are right that the Goldwater-Nichols Act played an important role in streamlining command authority in the U.S. military, and they make an interesting observation that America's devotion to the rule of law made it possible to completely transform our command structure between 1986 and 1991. They're also right that the challenges of modern warfare made the old structure—with each service branch having an independent chain of command up to its own chief of staff—dangerously inadequate. In a high-tech conflict like Desert Storm, we needed one commanding officer who was fully empowered to coordinate units of the Army, Navy, Air Force, and Marines. General Schwarzkopf filled that role brilliantly and set the precedent for future combatant commanders, who would need to get the various service branches working in harmony in Afghanistan and the 2003 invasion of Iraq, among other episodes.

In hindsight, Goldwater-Nichols or similar legislation should have gone even further to prepare the United States for the coming age of unrestricted warfare. The unification of the military service branches can be a role model for a more unified national response to the diverse range of threats posed by the CCP and other opponents, such as Iran and North Korea. We need a clearer, more cohesive structure to coordinate the nation's military, economic, diplomatic, and technological responses to unrestricted warfare.

China under Xi Jinping has recently enforced a similar reorganization of the People's Liberation Army. I saw this firsthand as I negotiated the return of the unmanned underwater vehicle (UUV) that the PLA navy stole from the United States in the South China Sea. While it appeared that the Chinese ship's captain might have acted outside his authority (he grabbed the vessel in plain view of the U.S. warship sent to retrieve it), the PLA's redesigned command-and-control system ensured that Xi had full knowledge as the crisis unfolded.

I spent a long night in the company of the Chinese general in charge of Russian military relations, because the general responsible for the U.S. military relationship was traveling abroad. I witnessed how orders were passed directly from the Central Military Commission, where Xi presided as chairman. The PLA was able to send pictures of the UUV back to the CMC, and the CMC was able to relay orders and intent to the ship.

What the authors of *UW* had grasped in 1998 was the potential for technology to directly connect leaders to front-line troops. Xi would later use this knowledge and American technology to create a world-class, high-tech system that enables perfect control of the PLA's actions, thus preserving the CCP leadership's authority where it matters most. What Xi did not want was a military confrontation that could inhibit trade, investment, and technology coming from the West. After the UUV crisis was successfully averted, the PLA's U.S. military representative told me, "We do not want confrontation now. It is not part of our strategy."

GOING FURTHER THAN AIR-LAND BATTLE

... *The actual battlefield conditions were quite a bit different from what people had envisioned beforehand. "Desert Storm" was basically an "all-air," no-"ground" campaign that lasted several dozen days, and they barely got to use "Desert Sword," which was displayed at the last moment, including that beautiful "left hook," for only 100 hours before wrapping things up in a huff. The ground war ... was like a concerto which winds up hastily after the first movement is played. Douhet's* [Italian Gen. Giulio Douhet, air war theorist in the 1920s] *prediction that "the battlefield in the air will be the decisive one" seems to have achieved belated confirmation. However, everything that happened in the air over the Gulf far exceeded the imagination of this proponent of achieving victory through the air. Whether in Kuwait or Iraq, none of the air combat involved gallant duels for air supremacy, but represented an integrated air campaign that blended all the combat operations, such as reconnaissance, early-warning, bombing, dogfights, communications, electronic strikes, and command*

and control, etc., together, and it also included the struggle for and occupation of outer space and cyberspace.

At this point, the Americans who proposed the "Air-land battle" concept have already gone quite a bit further than Douhet, but even so, they will still have to wait several years before they understand that, once they resort to the theory of integrated operations in real combat, the scope will go far beyond what they initially envisioned, extending over a broad and all-inclusive range that covers the ground, sea, air, space, and cyber realms. . . . [The Gulf War] is destined to become the starting point for the theory of "omni-dimensional" combat proposed by the elite of the U.S Army when they suddenly woke up. . . .

Not only that, but the "air tasking order" also provided a model for a kind of organizational command for all subsequent combat operations. One "order" represented an optimal scheme for combining the combat forces among the service arms, and the complexity and success of its trans-national combinations was where it really shone. In this respect alone, it was already far beyond the range of what was envisioned by the architects of the "Air-land battle" theory. This is to say that the U.S. unintentionally ushered the God of War into an open area in which she had never set foot.

This section and the next explain the colonels' conclusion that air war has become dominant over land war, just as Douhet had predicted. In fact, the suddenness of air power's dramatic success relative to land power caught the American military establishment by surprise. We spent the years after Desert Storm failing to appreciate the new value of air power—not merely in direct combat but also in what the colonels call "communications, electronic strikes, . . . outer space and cyberspace"—all of which are key areas of unrestricted warfare. While the United States saw the success of air power in Desert Storm as an anomaly, the CCP saw it as a key lesson, one they applied to their new, high-tech military.

WHO IS THE KING OF LAND WARFARE?

... Although the U.S. Army used helicopters to smash the Iraqi armored and mechanized units, once the gunsmoke in the Gulf cleared it inexplicably reverted to its pre-war level of thinking, shunting aside the helicopters which by all rights should have been the new favorites in the war. It is said that during the entire ground war, other than one desperate fight put up by the "Medina" armored division of the Republican Guard when it was surrounded south of Basra by the U.S. VII Corps, there was hardly any tank warfare worthy of the name. However, the Americans ... increased development outlays for other weapons, including tanks, while appropriations for helicopters was the only thing cut back. Sticking to their outmoded ways, they are still treating tanks as the decisive weapon in future ground warfare.

Actually, as early as the Vietnam war, helicopters had begun to display their abilities in the hands of the Americans, and soon afterward, the Soviet Union let helicopters show their exceptional skills in the hilly regions of Afghanistan, as did the British in the Falkland Islands. However, because their opponents were mainly guerrillas and non-armored infantry, it delayed the challenge that helicopters would pose to tanks a full 20 years. The Gulf War finally gave helicopters an opportunity to show what they could do. This time, not counting the helicopter units of the allied forces, the U.S. military alone deployed 1,600 helicopters of various models to the Gulf, and this enormous group of helicopters was sufficient to form one complete helicopter army. However, at this time the Americans, who had all along boasted of their innovative spirit, showed no originality at all, but . . . had the helicopters serve as a force attached to the armored and mechanized units and other troops. . . .

Just as the Americans were praising the "Patriot", the F-117, the "Tomahawk" missiles, and other battlefield stars to the skies via CNN, the helicopters were unfairly given the cold shoulder (with just the "Apache," which was a favorite, getting passing marks). Other than the "Final Report to Congress" written by the Department of Defense after the war, very few people still recall that it was the helicopters, not some of the other favorite new weapons, that performed first-rate service in Desert Storm. . . .

The . . . helicopters used "Hellfire" missiles to carry out advance destruction of Iraqi early-warning radar, opening a safe passage for the bomber groups and showing the incomparable penetration capabilities of helicopters. As the most flexible flying platform on the battlefield, they also undertook a large number of the supply transport, medical evacuation, search and rescue, battlefield reconnaissance, and electronic countermeasures missions. . . . This was definitely the most deeply significant tactical operation of the ground war during the war. It proclaimed that, from this point, helicopters were perfectly capable of conducting large-scale operations independently.

When the throngs of Iraqi soldiers ran from the fortifications destroyed by the helicopters and knelt to beg to surrender, they were in turn herded into a group by the helicopters, just like a cattle drive on the Western plains, and the view that "only the infantry can ultimately resolve a battle" has now been radically shaken by these American "flying cowboys." Originally, however, the initial intent of the leapfrog operation by the helicopters was just to provide support for the armored units that were to handle the main offensive, but the unexpected success of the helicopter units caused the plan to fall far behind the developments in the battle situation.... To this day, there has still been no example of combat which has demonstrated that any kind of tanks can keep up with the combat pace of helicopters....

In fact, tanks and helicopters are natural enemies, but the former is far from a match for the latter, and even the outmoded AH-1 "Cobra" helicopters, not to mention the AH-64 "tank-killer" helicopters, destroyed upwards of 100 tanks during the Gulf War while sustaining no casualties at all of their own. Faced with the powerful strike capabilities of the helicopters, who can still maintain that "the best weapon to deal with tanks are tanks?"

We can now say that helicopters are the true tank terminators. This new star, which rose gradually over the waves of the Gulf, is in the process of achieving its own coronation through the illustrious battle achievements during the Gulf War, and there is no doubt that it is just a question of time before it drives the tank from the battlefield....

Once again, I have to admit that these Chinese colonels saw things more clearly than our own leaders at the Pentagon. After Desert Storm, our continued overinvestment in tanks and underinvestment in helicopters showed our failure to grapple honestly with the lessons of that war. High-tech helicopters can now fill most of the role of tanks while having a great advantage in combat against tanks. Denying this fact reflected the Pentagon's stubbornness, its reluctance to study mistakes after a victory, and its general conservativism when it comes to changing strategy. All of these traits would soon have far more serious repercussions in the face of China's stealth war in the years after Desert Storm.

While unrestricted warfare is mostly about defeating your enemy without fighting, the colonels recognized useful military lessons as well. When the CCP eventually decides to invade Taiwan, they will apply these lessons. I expect the heavy use of air power to include helicopters, not the vast naval armada envisioned by the Pentagon's naval strategists. The attack will be swift and overwhelming, providing little time to respond. One major lesson of Desert Storm for the PLA was that a well-planned and well-executed air campaign is almost impossible to defeat.

ANOTHER PLAYER HIDDEN BEHIND THE VICTORY

... In terms of the CNN television broadcasts, the whole world was the same as the U.S. president in that they saw at the same time the soul-stirring start of the war. In the information-sharing age, a president doesn't really have much more in the way of special privileges than an ordinary citizen. This is where modern warfare differs from any wars of the past, with real-time or near real-time reports turning warfare into a new program that ordinary people can monitor directly via the media, and thus the media has become an immediate and integral part of warfare, and no longer merely provides information coming from the battlefield.

Unlike a direct broadcast of a World Cup soccer match, everything that people saw, other than that which was first limited by the subjective perspective of the television reporters (the 1300 reporters sent to the front lines were all aware of the "Revised Regulations Re-

garding Gulf War News Reports" issued by the Pentagon, so each person in his own mind exercised restraint about what could and could not be reported), also had to go through security reviews at the joint news offices set up in Dhahran and Riyadh. Perhaps U.S. military circles and the media had both learned the lesson during the Vietnam war when the discord between the two was so great, but this time the news agencies and the military got along very well. . . .

The U.S. press uniformly abandoned its vaunted neutrality, enthusiastically joining the anti-Iraq camp and coordinating with the U.S. military just like an outstanding two-man comic act, quite tacitly and energetically arriving at the same script for the war, with the force of the media and that of the allied army forming a joint force regarding the attack on Iraq. Not long after Iraq invaded Kuwait, reports quickly appeared in the various media that a massive U.S. force was streaming into Saudi Arabia, causing the Iraqi military on the Kuwait-Saudi Arabia border to flinch and quietly creating the momentum for a "hobbling" operation.

The day before the start of "Desert Storm," the Western media again trumpeted the news of a U.S. carrier fleet passing through the Suez Canal, which served to confuse Saddam and have him believe that, with disaster looming, the U.S. forces had still not completed their deployment. Similarly, without the support of the embellishment by the media, none of the so-called high-tech weapons sent to be used in the Gulf War would have been as awesome as people believed. In the upwards of 98 press conferences held throughout the entire course of the war, people saw images of how the precision-guided missiles could penetrate the air vents in a building and explode, of "Patriots" intercepting "Scuds," and numerous other shots that left a profound *impression. All these things represented an intense visual shock to the entire world, including the Iraqis, and it was from this that the myth about the unusual powers of the U.S.-made weapons was born, and it was here that the belief was formed that "Iraq would inevitably lose, and the U.S. was bound to win." Obviously, the media helped the Americans enormously. We might as well say that, intentionally or otherwise, the U.S. military and the Western media joined hands to form a noose to hang Saddam's Iraq from the gallows. In the "Operational Outline" that was revised after the war, the Americans took pains to suggest that "the force of the media reports was able to have a dramatic effect on the strategic direction and the scope of the military operations." . . . It would appear that, in all future wars, in addition to the basic method of military strikes, the force of the media will increasingly be another player in the war and will play a role comparable to that of military strikes in promoting the course of the war.*

Unlike battlefield propaganda, which has an excessively subjective tinge and is easily rejected by an opponent or by neutral individuals, because it is cleverly cloaked as objective reporting the media has a quiet impact that is hard to gauge. In the Gulf, in the same manner that the U.S.-led allied forces deprived Iraq of its right to speak militarily, the powerful Western media deprived it politically of its right to speak, to defend itself, and even of its right to sympathy and support, and compared to the weak voice of Iraqi propaganda, which portrayed Bush as the "great Satan" who was wicked beyond redemption, the image of Saddam as a war-crazed aggressor was played up in a much more convincing fashion. It was precisely the lopsided media force together with the lopsided military force that dealt a vicious one-

two blow to Iraq on the battlefield and morally, and this sealed Sad-dam's defeat.

However, the effects of the media have always been a two-edged sword. This means that, while it is directed at the enemy, at the same time on another front it can similarly be a sharp sword directed at oneself. Based on information that was disclosed following the war, the reason that the ground war abruptly came to a halt after 100 hours was actually because Bush, influenced by a hasty assessment of the course of the war that was issued on television by a battlefield news release officer, later came to a similarly hasty decision of his own, "dramatically shortening the time from strategic decision-making to concluding the war." As a result, Saddam, whose days were numbered, escaped certain death. . . .

The impact of the media on warfare is becoming increasingly widespread and increasingly direct, to the point where even major decisions by the president of a superpower such as this one involving the cessation of hostilities are to a very great extent rooted in the reaction to a single television program. From this, one can perceive a bit of the significance that the media carries in social life today. One can say entirely without exaggeration that an uncrowned king has now become the major force to win any battle. After "Desert Storm" swept over the Gulf, no longer would it be possible to rely on military force alone without the involvement of the media to achieve victory in a war.

This section, on the role of the media, is especially important for understanding the CCP's development of unrestricted warfare. Coverage of the Gulf War by the U.S. media was shockingly different from the Vietnam and post–Vietnam eras, roughly 1965–1990. Instead of challenging and doubting official statements about our military objectives and outcomes, most of those 1,300 credentialed and embedded journalists delivered positive coverage about nearly every aspect of Desert Storm. The authors of *UW* may exaggerate just how much the American media abandoned its commitment to objectivity and neutrality, but it certainly felt like they were on the side of our armed forces, perhaps for the first time since World War II.

Any American old enough to watch CNN in 1991 will recall amazingly clear and immediate footage of the Gulf War. We saw precision-targeted bombs going down the ventilator shafts and into the windows of Iraqi military targets, such as munitions factories, as well as Patriot missiles taking out Iraqi Scud missiles. Civilians in the United States also watched sympathetic interviews with deployed troops, as well as with JCS chairman Colin Powell and the commanding general of the Central Command and all coalition forces, "Stormin' Norman" Schwarzkopf. Both generals became national celebrities in a way that would have been unthinkable a decade earlier. As the colonels note, all of this positive media coverage didn't merely boost the war's popularity in the United States; it also affected real-time decisions by our allies and by the Iraqis themselves. It made America's success seem even more decisive and inevitable.

The Chinese drew a key lesson about the power of modern media, especially cable TV news with satellite hookups able to broadcast from and to any corner of the world. Friendly media coverage can have more influence than any government-produced propaganda, precisely because it comes across as objective. The CCP would work hard not only to control what Chinese citizens saw and heard on official state media, but also to influence what the rest of the world saw and heard from supposedly objective Western outlets. Those outlets could be subtly influenced by being given appealing narratives and visuals that they would gladly share with their audiences. Or the CCP could own a large share of the conglomerates that control the producers of the news. With today's corporate consolidation of media and news organizations, it's easy for the CCP to build up large ownership stakes that give them influence at major media outlets.

AN APPLE WITH NUMEROUS SECTIONS

As a war characterized by the integration of technology that concluded the old era and inaugurated the new one, "Desert Storm" is a classic war that can provide all-encompassing inspiration to those in the military in every country. Any person who enjoys delving into military issues can invariably draw some enlightenment or lessons from this war, regardless of which corner of the war one focuses on. Based on that, we are terming this war, which has multiple meanings with regard to its experiences and lessons, a multi-section apple. Furthermore, the sectional views of this apple are far from being limited to those that we have already discussed, and it is only necessary for one to approach it with a well-honed intellect to have an unexpected sectional view appear before one's eyes at any moment:

When President Bush spoke with righteous indignation to the United States and the whole world about the moral responsibility being undertaken for Kuwait, no responsible economist could have predicted that, to provide for the military outlays of this war, the

United States would propose a . . . "shared responsibility" program, thereby launching a new form for sharing the costs of international war—fighting together and splitting the bill. Even if you aren't a businessman, you have to admire this kind of Wall Street spirit.

Psychological warfare is really not a new tactic, but what was novel about the psychological warfare in "Desert Storm" was its creativity. After dropping an extremely powerful bomb, they would then have the airplanes drop propaganda leaflets, warning the Iraqi soldiers several kilometers away who were quaking in their boots from the bombing that the next bomb would be their turn! This move alone was sufficient to cause the Iraqi units which were organized in divisions to collapse. In the prisoner of war camp, one Iraqi division commander admitted that the impact of the psychological war on Iraqi morale was second only to the bombing by the allied forces. . . .

We will see that there are even more aspects to this apple, but not all of them are by any means things that can be pointed out or circled everywhere. To tell the truth, its flaws and questionable aspects are nearly as numerous as its strengths, but nonetheless this cannot cause us to treat it with the slightest contempt. Although this was a war rich with implications, it still cannot be treated as the encyclopedia of modern warfare, at least it does not provide us with any completely ready-made answers regarding future warfare. However, it does represent the first and most concentrated use of a large number of new and advanced weapons since their appearance, as well as a testing ground for the revolution in military affairs. . . . This point is sufficient to earn it the position of a classic in the history of warfare, as well as providing a completely new hotbed for our budding thoughts.

The colonels wrap up by noting that for all of the Gulf War's military, diplomatic, technological, and media innovations, they refused to assume that it would be a blueprint for future wars. They accurately saw it as a unique episode at the intersection of multiple trends that might never again line up the same way. Sure enough, when the United States returned to combat in the Middle East a decade later, in the wake of 9/11, so much was different, from our advantages on the battlefield to the attitude of the media.

Nevertheless, the CCP gave this "multi-section apple" more careful scrutiny and analysis than the Pentagon did, drawing many accurate insights about future international conflicts. Their biggest takeaway was that it made no sense for China to get into any kind of conventional military engagement against the United States, because its forces would surely be destroyed as completely as Saddam Hussein's. Trying to build better helicopters, bombs, or missiles would be futile, achieving nothing except draining China's treasury. In part because of these warnings by the colonels about conventional war, the CCP redirected its resources and efforts into the many economic, diplomatic, and psychological tactics of a new kind of warfare without rules.

As they write in the next section, the United States did not follow such an expansive path. Extending their critique of the Gulf War, they note that U.S. military strategists considered the notion of noncombat warfare, but went for more hardware instead.

CHAPTER 7

AMERICA'S WEAKNESS

OUR ABRUPT AND BADLY MANAGED WITHDRAWAL FROM Afghanistan in the summer of 2021 was necessitated, as President Biden said, by an aversion to losing "one more American soldier." He insisted on this despite the advice of military advisers that keeping a small force was worth the risk. The Chinese propagandists had a field day mocking our humiliating retreat. The cause and effect was something the colonels predicted more than two decades ago when they identified the threat of casualties as a fundamental American weakness that could be exploited.

Gulf War Two happened four years after the colonels published their book, but its mismanagement and heavy price in lives and dollars is something they could have predicted. It started with the same high-tech intensity of the first Gulf War, routing Saddam Hussein's overmatched army in short order. It was what came next that was the tragedy. Guerrilla war—asynchronous, in Pentagon jargon—boiled up from the fanatical remnants of the Iraqi army along with what the colonels would call "non-state" actors. Their main mission was to kill U.S. soldiers—to create a body count that the U.S. public would not tolerate. It almost worked.

The colonels would argue, as they essentially do in this chapter, that many of the casualties of Iraq would have been avoidable if the United States had understood the new rules of war.

As diligent students of the American military, they take an after-action look at the first Gulf War and find some major missed opportunities on the part of the United States. They marvel at the cost of the war in dollars and conclude that we did not take away the proper lessons for reforming our military capacity. This "battle banquet" featuring bombers that are virtually a "flying mountain of gold," they write, has made us arrogant while exposing some fundamental weaknesses to our enemies. Prime among them, a fear of battlefield casualties.

Remember, these are military men, writing first to a military audience. They display a deep understanding of the policy debates that have raged in the Pentagon and the congressional committees and offer their clear criticism with a level of detail that I would have been happy to have seen presented at a contentious Pentagon session.

From Chapter 4 of *Unrestricted Warfare*

THE ILLNESS OF EXTRAVAGANCE, AND ZERO CASUALTIES

Large-scale use of costly weapons in order to realize objectives and reduce casualties without counting costs—the kind of warfare that can only be waged by men of wealth—is a game that the American

*military is good at. "Desert Storm" manifested the Americans' unlim-
ited extravagance in war, which has already become an addiction.
Airplanes which cost an average of US$25 million each carried out
11,000 wanton and indiscriminate bombings in a 42-day period, destroying the headquarters of Iraq's Socialist Party with each US$1.3
million Tomahawk guided missile, taking aim at foxholes with precision guided bombs worth tens of thousands of U.S. dollars ... even if
the American generals knew as soon as they began that they need not
spend so much on this unrestrained US$61 billion battle banquet, ...
their over-extravagance would still not have been prevented. An
American-made bomber is like a flying mountain of gold, more costly
than many of its targets. Shouldn't hitting a possibly insignificant target with tons of American dollars arouse people's suspicions?*

*Aside from this, during the long duration of 161 days, more than
52,000 personnel and over 8,000,000 tons of goods and materials were
brought over day and night to the front line from America and all over
Europe, including thousands of sun hats long since scrapped in some
warehouse and crates of American fruit rotting [in] Riyadh. ... Of all
the soldiers in the world, probably only the Americans would consider
this a necessary extravagance in order to win one war. ...*

*Even the Armed Services Committee of the House of Representa-
tives, an organization that frequently conducts verbal warfare with
four star generals over money, did not even utter a word regarding
the astonishing expenditures of this war. In the respective investigation reports done on the Gulf War, the key effect of high technology
weaponry was given almost all equally high appraisals. Secretary
of Defense Cheney said "we lead fully one generation in the area of
weapon technology," and Congressman Aspen responded "the benefits*

*demonstrated by high tech weaponry have exceeded our most opti-
mistic estimates."...*

*This is a nationality that has never been willing to pay the price
of life and, moreover, has always vied for victory at all costs. The appearance of high technology weaponry can now satisfy these extravagant hopes of the American people. During the Gulf War, of 500,000
troops, there were only 148 fatalities and 458 wounded.... Ever since
the Vietnam War, both the military and American society have been
sensitized to human casualties during military operations, almost to
the point of morbidity. Reducing casualties and achieving war objectives have become the two equal weights on the American military
scale. These common American soldiers who should be on the battlefield have now become the costliest security in war, like precious china
bowls that people are afraid to break. All of the opponents who have
engaged in battle with the American military have probably mastered
the secret of success—if you have no way of defeating this force, you
should kill its rank and file soldiers. This point, taken from the U.S.
Congressional report's emphasis on "reducing casualties is the highest objective in formulating the plan," can be unequivocally confirmed.
"Pursuit of zero casualties," this completely compassionate simple
slogan, has actually become the principal motivating factor in creating American style extravagant warfare....*

*Warfare framed on this basis can only be like killing a chicken
with a bull knife. Its high technology, high investment, high expendi-
ture, and high payback features make its requirements for military
strategy and combat skill far lower than its requirements for the technological performance of weaponry.... Compared with the advanced
technology that they possess, the American military clearly is techno-*

logically stagnant and it is not good at seizing opportunities provided by new technology for new military tactics. Aside from effective use of advanced technological weaponry, we are not sure how much of a disparity exists between the military thought revealed in this war by Americans and other countries. The difference at least cannot be any bigger than that between their weaponry. Perhaps it is precisely because of this that this war was unable to become a masterpiece of military skill. Instead it became, to a great extent, a sumptuous international fair of high technology weapons with the United States as the representative and, as a result, began the spread of the disease of American style war extravagance on a global scale....

As the world's leading arms dealers, Americans naturally are overjoyed.... For a long time after the war people could not understand the main threads of this complicated affair and believed that modern warfare is fought in just this way, leaving those who cannot fight such an extravagant war feeling inadequate. This is why the military forums in every country since the Gulf War are full of a faction yearning for high technology weapons and calling for high technology wars.

In discussing the talented American inventor, Thomas Edison, poet [John Robinson] *Jeffers writes, "We ... are skilled in machinery and are infatuated with luxuries." Americans have a strong inborn penchant for these two things as well as a tendency to turn their pursuit of the highest technology and its perfection into a luxury, even including weapons and machinery.... This inclination makes them rigidly infatuated with ... technology and weapons, always thinking that the road to getting the upper hand with war can be found with technology and weapons. This inclination also makes them anxious at any given time that their own leading position in the realm of weaponry is wavering, and they continually alleviate these concerns by manufacturing more, newer, and more complex weapons.*

As a result of this attitude, when the weapons systems come into conflict with the terse principles required of actual combat, they always stand on the side of the weapons. They would rather treat war as the opponent in the marathon race of military technology and are not willing to look at it more as a test of morale and courage, wisdom and strategy.... Self confidence such as this has made them forget one simple fact—it is not so much that war follows the rivalry of technology and weaponry as it is a game field with continually changing direction and many irregular factors....

It appears that Americans, however, do not plan to pay attention to this. They drew the benefit of the Gulf War's technological victory and obviously have resolutely spared no cost to safeguard their leading position in high technology. Even though the many difficulties with funding have brought them up against the embarrassment of having difficulty continuing, they have not been able to change their passion for new technology and new weapons. The detailed list of extravagant weapons constantly being drawn up by the U.S. military and approved by Congress will certainly get longer and longer, but the list of American soldier casualties in future wars may not necessarily be "zero" because of wishful thinking.

The Pentagon's obsession with reducing casualties goes back to the Vietnam War. Every night on the evening news, millions of Americans heard the latest body count statistics and watched images of the caskets holding our dead troops. The relentless barrage of bad news, month after month through the late 1960s, drove public opinion sharply against the war and its leaders. During the post–Vietnam reckoning with what went wrong, and especially during the Reagan administration, the Pentagon set out to master high-tech weaponry that could help us win future wars quickly and overwhelmingly, with far fewer casualties.

The upside of this approach was the amazingly low casualty rate of the Gulf War. The downside, as the colonels note, is that it made it very clear to our adversaries that the easiest way to drive the United States out of a military conflict was to inflict high casualty rates on our troops, even if there was no strategic or tactical reason to do so. This scenario played out in Gulf War Two, where Saddam's forces were again routed with the brilliant deployment of high-tech weapons—only to see us bog down in a costly guerrilla insurgency that took much of its grisly toll on U.S. forces with primitive roadside bombs, the aptly named improvised explosive devices. The retaking of Iraq, from Fallujah to, finally, Mosul, required very old-school street fighting and a good dose of what the colonels called *morale and courage, wisdom and strategy.* But when it came to Afghanistan, where military technology has stark limits, we were no longer willing to pay the price of casualties. The Taliban knew that, bided their time by picking at our forces until we said "enough," and essentially retook the country. In both cases, I believe the colonels must be satisfied with the outcome of their predictions.

Whether it is blood or treasure, the colonels say that the American military has invented an extremely expensive way to go to war, and one that can be exploited. If we pursue this path with vigor, it will likely lead to further draining America's coffers. Not lost on the two colonels was how the United States won the Cold War. We didn't bomb the Soviet Union, we bankrupted them. Interestingly, this is also a theme featured in Osama bin Laden's strategy—spark a war and bankrupt the West. In the CCP's case, take advantage of other adversaries (Iran, Russia, North Korea) to keep American military forces distracted and defense budgets correspondingly high. Eventually, like the Soviets', the U.S. economy would collapse as infrastructure, scientific research, and STEM education are left unfunded as the United States spends more and more on defense.

FROM JOINT CAMPAIGNS TO
TOTAL DIMENSIONAL WAR

... *The "new military revolution"*... [has] *become a blindly ludicrous and popular slogan.* .... *If* [the Americans] *want to guarantee their own leading position in a field of military reforms that has already begun and will be completed right away, then the first thing that must be resolved is to eliminate the lag between U.S. military thinking and military technology.* .... *They have achieved certain results that are equally beneficial for American servicemen as well as servicemen all over the world—first is formation of the "joint campaign" concept, second is forging "total dimensional warfare" thinking.*

Formulation of the "joint campaign" originally came from the Number One Joint Publication in November 1991 of the "United States Armed Forces Joint Operations" regulations issued by the U.S. Military Joint Conference. .... *This regulation exposes the four key elements of* the *"joint campaign"—centralized command, equality of the armed forces, complete unification, and total depth while doing battle. It has made clear for the first time the command control authority of the battle zone unified commander; it has stipulated that any one military branch can take the leading battle role based on different situations; it has expanded "air/ground integrated battle" into ground, sea, air, and space integrated battle; and it has emphasized implementation of total depth while doing battle on all fronts. ...*

The limitation of this valuable thinking, however, lies in that its starting point and ending point have both fallen onto the level of armed force and have been unable to expand the field of vision of "joint" to all of the realms in which humans can produce confrontational behavior. The drawback of this thinking ... at a time when an inkling of the broad sense of war has already emerged, is that it appears to attract attention to such an extent that if the concept of "total dimensional warfare" had not been set forth in the 1993 U.S. Army publication, The Essentials of War, we would be astounded at the "anemic" realm of U.S. military thinking.

Following the 13th revision of this document, there was a penetrating insight into the various challenges that the U.S. military might face in the following years and for the first time a completely new concept of "non-combat military operations" was advanced. It was because of this concept that people saw the possibility of carrying out total positional warfare, and it brought the American Army to find an extremely lofty new name for its war theory—"total dimensional warfare." What is interesting is that the person in charge of revising The Essentials of War and who displayed a fiercely innovative spirit was

General [Tommy] *Franks, the man who was criticized by people as an operational conservative when the Navy commanded the Seventh Fleet....*

General Franks and the officers who compiled his military regulations were unable to reconcile the tremendous discrepancy between two sentences—"implementation of centralized air, ground and sea operations supported by the entire theatre of operations" and "mobilization of all mastered methods in each possible operation, both combat and non-combat, so as to resolutely complete any mission assigned at the least price"—in ... The Essentials of War. They were even less able to discover that, apart from war as a military operation, there still exists the possibility for far vaster non-military war operations....

It is too bad that the Americans, or more specifically the American Army, discontinued this revolution too early.... [Lieutenant General Holder's] *view was that "the belief that non-combat operations has its own set of principles is not welcomed among combat troops, and many commanding officers are opposed to differentiating between non-combat operations and the original meaning of military operations." After Holder's death, "the Army had formed a common consensus to handle differentiation of non-combat operations as a wrong practice." They believe that if "non-combat military operations" are written into the basic regulations, it will weaken the armed forces' trait of emphasis on military affairs and also could lead to confusion in armed forces operations. With the situation going in this direction, General Franks' revolution ended in an unavoidable miscarriage. Under the inspiration of the next commander of the Army Training and Doctrine Headquarters, General Hartzog, General Holder and*

142

the editorial group for the 1998 edition of The Essentials of War finally made a major amendment to the new compendium with "a single principle covering all types of the Army's military operations" as the fundamental key. Their practice is to no longer distinguish between non-combat operations and general military operations, but to differentiate battle operations into four types—attack, defense, stabilization, and support—and return the original manuscript to such responsibilities of non-combat operations as rescue and protection and reassembling the old set of combat operations, in order to . . . altogether discard the concept of "total dimensional warfare."

At face value, this is a move of radical reform and simplification by simply cutting out the superfluous. In reality, however, this is . . . poor judgment. At the same time as the theoretical confusion brought by the unripe concept of "non-combat military operations" was eliminated, the rather valuable ideological fruits that they had accidentally picked were also abandoned on account of the newly-revised compendium. . . .

"Total dimensional war's" understanding of battle is already much broader than any previous military theory, but as far as its innate character is concerned, it still has not escaped the "military" category. For example, the "non-military combat operations" concept . . . is much broader in meaning than military combat operations and can be placed along with comparable war realms and patterns outside the field of vision of American servicemen. It is precisely this large domain that is the area for future servicemen and politicians to develop imagination and creativity—with the result that it also cannot count as truly meaning "total dimensional." . . .

No one ... can launch a war in 360-degree three-dimensional space with time and other non-physical elements of total dimensionality added, and any particular war will always have its particular emphasis and is always launched within a limited dimension.... The only difference is that in the predictable future, military operations will never again be the entire war, rather they are one dimension within the total dimension. Even adding "non-combat military operations" as proposed by General Franks cannot count as total dimensionality. Only by adding all "non-military combat operations" aside from military operations can total dimensional war's complete significance be realized.... Even though these concepts of "non-combat military operations" and "total dimensional warfare" are full of original ideas and are already fairly close to a military ideological revolution ... the mountain peak of the great revelation is still far away. Here, however, the Americans have stopped, and the American hares who have always been ahead of every other country in the world in military technology and military ideology have begun to gasp for breath....

Perhaps now this is the time when Lieutenant Colonel Lonnie Henley and these Americans who have called into question the capability of other countries' military revolutions should examine their consciences:

Why has there not been a revolution?

The colonels are tweaking the Pentagon again for being so proud of "revolutionary" military reforms that turned out to be not so revolutionary after all, because the Americans "discontinued this revolution too early." Joint campaign coordination among the various service branches and "total dimensional warfare" were both good ideas, but they didn't go nearly far enough toward the broader concept of unrestricted warfare. The authors believe that the United States missed a huge opportunity after the Gulf War to take the lead in unrestricted warfare and that our continued focus on conventional warfare in conventional battle spaces was a serious mistake. It's hard to disagree with their conclusion that there was already evidence in the 1990s that future wars would go far beyond land, sea, air, and even cyberspace.

Lonnie Henley was a career intelligence officer and China specialist who served twenty-two years in the U.S. Army after graduating from West Point. He then spent seventeen years in the senior civil service, including two tours as defense intelligence officer for East Asia. I met him at the Pentagon in 2014 when I worked for the Joint Chiefs of Staff. I have to agree that he was very conventional in his thinking about China and his underestimation of the CCP's overall threat, beyond its traditional military capacity.

The biggest point in this section is that just considering warfare from the point of view of the application of military force is insufficient. The president has numerous levers of power under his control, which can easily lead to overreliance on military options, as I witnessed when I was a member of the Joint Staff.

One good example was China's aggressive moves in the South China Sea in 2016–17, after the International Court of Justice at The Hague ruled in favor of the Philippines and against China's claims in the area. China rejected the ruling and continued to flex its might, a clear threat to Taiwan and others in the region. President Obama wanted the DOD to do something about it, but what could we do? Bomb them? We settled for sending our warships to the South China Sea to sail figure eights around the disputed small islands where the PLA was building full-fledged military bases—after they had denied any plans to build those bases. Perhaps the president should have asked the Treasury Department to stop allowing U.S. retirement funds to finance the building of the islands by buying stock in the China Communications Construction Company's dredging unit. That would have countered unrestricted warfare with unrestricted warfare.

At the end of the day, our system is still geared to leaning on the military and hard power as our best deterrent. That leaves the rest of the playing field open to the Chinese way of war.

CHAPTER 8

WEAPONIZING THE INTERNATIONAL ORDER

IN HIS 2020 PRESIDENTIAL MEMOIR, BARACK OBAMA OFFERS a candid and realistic view of dealing with China. He got what they were up to, he just didn't have a good response. He wrote how China had been "evading, bending, or breaking just about every agreed-upon rule of international commerce during its 'peaceful rise.'" He cited their "disregard for labor and environmental standards," and the "theft of U.S. intellectual property." Their currency manipulation and trade dumping undercut U.S. manufacturing. Their leaders were purely transactional with no regard for international law. "Where they met no resistance, they'd keep on taking."

He knew this behavior had gone on for many years, yet the response from Washington had been surprisingly "mild." He had the cynical understanding that the inaction of his predecessors was largely because from Wall Street to the farm belt, "There was too much money to be made." He then goes on to explain his strategy: It is to "nudge China toward better behavior." His plan for a "pivot to Asia"—never really enacted—"wasn't to contain China or stifle its growth" but to strengthen the framework of international law. Yet despite this equally mild strategy, Obama thought the Chinese would be upset. "I doubted the Chinese would see it that way," he concluded. In fact, it didn't matter, because the Chinese didn't care about international law, which they were in the process of further undermining. So much for nudge.

The need for China to infiltrate and exert influence over international organizations is a major recommendation of the colonels. In the middle of the book, the colonels weave together an amalgam of concepts that don't flow together all that smoothly, but nonetheless make some predictions that loom large to this day. In Part Two and the subsequent Chapters 5 and 7 (Chapter 6 is a bizarre digression into numerology as it relates to historical battle formations) they talk about international organizations and international terrorism both creating a world beyond the reach of sovereign nations— they call them "supra-national powers." And thus giving China a rationale to scrap the rules of civilized behavior. The arguments can be hard to follow, but the outcomes twenty years later are not.

This section treats the rise of multinational organizations as a strategy that countries were already using as nontraditional warfare. It returns to an argument we've seen repeatedly in *UW*—that China isn't really the bad guy because the Western powers have already been practicing their own forms of unrestricted warfare. The authors accuse the United States of weaponizing the international order, which justifies the Chinese Communist Party's systematic defiance of that order and the supposedly neutral organizations that represent and maintain it.

The colonels are really setting the table for China's aggressive entry into the globalized world. As of their writing, China didn't participate in—or was barred from—most international bodies. Whether to allow China into these organizations was a subject of intense debate among the world's wealthy countries. Eventually, they relented and China was prepared to make its move.

Over the past two decades, China has effectively orchestrated a takeover of the international institutions that the United States and its allies worked to build during the Cold War. Today, many of the leaders of UN organizations have been placed in their jobs, openly or stealthily, by the CCP. One example is Tedros Adhanom Ghebreyesus, director general of the World Health Organization. He was very helpful to the CCP in enabling China to hide the nature and origin of the coronavirus as it began to spread around the world. Then the WHO congratulated China for its use of lockdowns, thus encouraging democracies around the world to abandon civil liberties. Finally, the WHO whitewashed a report on the origin of the coronavirus by claiming there was no evidence that it came from a lab in Wuhan; more and more evidence now points to the contrary.

From Chapter 7 of *Unrestricted Warfare*

SUPRA-NATIONAL COMBINATIONS

. . . Modern countries are affected more and more by regional or world-wide organizations, such as the European Community [sic; now the European Union], ASEAN, OPEC, APEC, the International Monetary Fund, the World Bank, the WTO, and the biggest of them all, the

United Nations. Besides these, a large number of multinational orga-
nizations and non-state organizations of all shapes and sizes, such as
multinational corporations, trade associations, peace and environ-
mental organizations, the Olympic Committee, religious organizations,
terrorist organizations, small groups of hackers, etc., dart from left
and right into a country's path. These multinational, non-state, and
supra-national organizations together constitute an up and coming
worldwide system of power. . . .

[These] factors are leading us into an era of transformation in
which great power politics are yielding to supra-national politics. . . .
The curtain is now slowly falling on the era in which the final decision
on victory and defeat is made by way of state vs. state tests of strength.
Instead, the curtain is quietly opening on an era in which problems
will be resolved and objectives achieved by using supra-national
means on a stage larger than the size of a country. . . .

In this world of mutually penetrating political, economic, ideo-
logical, technical, and cultural influences, with networks, clones, Hol-
lywood, . . . internet pornography, and the World Cup easily bypassing
territorial boundary markers, it is very hard to realize hopes of assur-
ing security and pursuing interests in a purely national sense. Only a
fool like Saddam Hussein would seek to fulfill his own wild ambition
by outright territorial occupation. . . .

Except for small countries like Grenada and Panama, against
which it took direct and purely military action, in most situations the
United States now pursues and realizes its own interests by using
supra-national means. . . . During the entire course of their actions,
the Americans acted in collusion with others, maneuvering among
various political groups, and getting the support of practically all the

countries in the United Nations. The United States got this, the premier international organization in all the world, to issue a resolution to make trouble under a pretext provided by the United States, and dragged over 30 countries into the joint force sent against Iraq. After the war, the United States was again successful in organizing an economic embargo of Iraq which has continued for eight years, and it used arms inspections to maintain continuous political and military pressure on Iraq. This has left Iraq in long-term political isolation and dire economic straits. . . .

Worldwide economic integration, internationalization of domestic politics, the networking of information resources, . . . the concealment of cultural conflicts, and the strengthening of non-state organizations, all bring human society both convenience and troubles. This is why the great powers, and even some medium and small sized countries, act in concert without need of prior coordination and set their sights on supra-national combinations to solve their problems. . . .

As the world's only world-class superpower, the United States is the best at using supra-national combinations as a weapon. The United States never misses any opportunity to take a hand in international organizations involving U.S. interests. Another way to put it is that the United States consistently sees the actions of all international organizations as being closely related to U.S. interests. No matter whether the nature of the international organization is European, American, Asian, for some other region, or worldwide, the United States always strives to get involved in it, and manipulate it. . . .

For example, when the IMF extended a $57 billion loan to South Korea, it was with the condition that Korea must open up its markets *completely and allow American capital the opportunity to buy up Korean enterprises at unreasonably low prices. A demand such as this is armed robbery. It gives the developed countries, with the United States as their leader, the opportunity to gain unrestricted access to another country's markets, or to get in and clear out some space there. It is little different from a disguised form of economic occupation. . . .*

It's important to keep in mind that in 1999, China was still mostly excluded from powerful international organizations like the World Bank, the IMF, and the World Trade Organization. The CCP desperately wanted access to those organizations to boost its economy and take advantage of the internet-driven wave of globalization. But at the same time, the CCP held those organizations in contempt as alleged puppets of the United States—a means for us to exploit smaller countries during crises like the East Asian financial crash of 1998.

The CCP's contempt set the stage for two decades of lying to and manipulation of those organizations, once it got access. China also now invests enormous resources to influence emerging countries in Africa and South Asia, through tactics like the Belt and Road Initiative. Developing countries that receive Chinese infrastructure investment as part of the Belt and Road Initiative usually vote for whichever candidates the CCP supports at key international organizations—including Ghebreyesus at the WHO. Then, almost like magic, the UN and other key organizations have been making more and more decisions that favor the CCP.

In addition, the Chinese have been granted a significant portion of World Bank development loans despite being the world's second biggest economy. Their currency is part of the IMF basket despite the fact that it is not convertible and China has strict capital controls in place. It is part of the WTO despite the fact that it does not have a market economy. It is a member of the UN Human Rights Council despite committing genocide in Xinjiang. In effect, it has turned the international order built by the United States and its allies into a promoter of authoritarianism.

It's a corrupt world, the colonels argue, and so what? The next section walks through this strange confluence that puts the United Nations, George Soros, and Osama bin Laden in the same box and says: Learn from the successful actions of bad actors.

From Chapter 5 of *Unrestricted Warfare*

THE DESTRUCTION OF RULES AND
THE DOMAIN OF LOSING EFFECTIVENESS

As an extreme means for resolving conflicts of survival and interests, war has always been the beast truly tamed by mankind. . . . Over the last several thousand years, and especially in the 20th century, during the intervals between the fires of war, there . . . [have] always been efforts to lock the beast in the cage. It is for this reason that people have formulated innumerable treaties and rules. From the famous Geneva Convention to the United Nations to the present, they have begun to continuously make various resolutions concerning war, erected one railing after another on the roads of crazy and bloody wars, and have wanted to use international laws and regulations to control the harm of war to mankind. . . . [These include] not allowing the use of biochemical weapons, not allowing the indiscriminate killing [of] civilians, not allowing the mistreatment of prisoners, and limiting the use of land mines. . . .

At the conclusion of the Cold War, the entire world was over-joyed and considered that a "fearful peace" was being entered. After Schwarzkopf used a "storm" fist to down Saddam on the Gulf fighting stage, President Bush was elated with success: "The new order of the world has already withstood its first test." He was like Chamberlain returning from Munich announcing that mankind will "get together in a world having the hope of peace." What was the result? Like Chamberlain, he also boasted too early.

[Neither] *the end of the Cold War nor the Gulf War . . . was able to bring about the promises of politicians and a new international order anticipated by all of mankind. The collapse of the polarized world resulted in the beasts of local wars roaring out of their cages one by one drenching the nations and regions of Rwanda, Somalia, Bohei, Chechen, Congo, and Kosovo in pools of blood. People had again dis-covered by this time how the efforts for peace over several thousand years could collapse at one single blow!*

[This] *situation is related to the practical attitude embraced by each nation concerning the establishment of international rules. Whether or not each nation acknowledges the rules often depends on whether or not they are beneficial to themselves. Small nations hope to use the rules to protect their own interests, while large nations at-tempt to use the rules to control other nations. When the rules are not in accord with the interests of one's own nation, generally speaking, the breaking of the rules by small nations can be corrected by large nations in the name of enforcers of the law. However, when large na-tions break the rules, for example when the United States . . . grabbed the head of* [Panama, Manuel Noriega] *and brought him to be tried in their own nation . . . the international community . . . only sighed in despair, being at a loss of what to do. . . .*

In the international community, the participation by large nations, when facing the weak and powerless, in the formulation and the utilization of rules as well as the disregard and even destruction of rules when the rules are not advantageous to them, . . . contrast with . . . non-state forces who do not acknowledge any rules and specialize in taking the existing national order as their goal of destruction. . . . These non-state forces . . . both destroy the normal international order and restrain the destruction of the international community by those large nations. For example, there were the warning intrusions of nameless hackers to the web site of the National Defense Ministry of India after it carried out nuclear tests and the terrorist act by the rich Moslem Osama bin Laden because of his dissatisfaction with the presence of the United States in the Middle East. . . .

The direct result of the destruction of rules is that the domains delineated by visible or invisible boundaries by the international community lose effectiveness. [All] *principals without national power who employ non-military warfare actions against the international community use means that go beyond nations, regions and measures. Visible national boundaries, invisible internet space, international law, national law, behavioral norms, and ethical principles, have absolutely no restraining effects on them. They are not responsible to anyone, nor limited by any rules, and there is no disgrace when it comes to the selection of targets, nor are there any means not used. Owing to the surreptitious nature of their movements, they have very strong concealment, create widespread damage, . . . and appear unusually cruel due to their indiscriminate attacks on civilians. All of this is also broadcast in real time via continuous coverage by the modern media, which very much strengthens the effects of terrorism. When carrying out war with these people, there is no declaration of war, no fixed battlefield, no face-to-face fighting and killing, and in the majority of situations, there will be no gunpowder smoke, gun fire, and spilling of blood. However, the destruction and injuries encountered by the international community are in no way less than those of a military war.*

Following the gradual fading out of the old terrorists who specialized in kidnapping, assassination, and hijacking, new forces of terrorism quickly appeared and rapidly filled in the vacuum left by their predecessors. During a short period of ten years, they transformed from being persons of nameless origins to world public nuisances, with the chief among them being computer hackers. The popularization of personal computers, and especially the formation of the internet, has resulted in the malicious acts of hackers increasingly endangering the existing social order. . . . Faced with these prospects, even [the head of investigation of computer crimes in the FBI] *said . . . : "Give me ten carefully chosen hackers, and within 90 days I would then be able to have this nation lay down its arms and surrender."*

When compared with . . . these network terrorist hackers, the terror of the bombs of bin Laden are closer to the traditional terrorism in legacy. However, this does not prevent us from considering him to be within the ranks of new terrorism. . . . Prior to the major bombings at the American embassies in Nairobi and Dares Salaam which shocked the world, the name of bin Laden was still not listed in the name list of the 30 terrorist organizations published by the Interna-

tional Anti-Terrorist Organization, and even though he already had many murder cases attributed to him, he was only a "nameless hero" in the Islamic world, owing to his having not boasted of them. Even after the Americans had already launched cruise missiles at him and issued an arrest warrant, he still repeatedly denied that he was personally connected with the bombing cases. "Concealing oneself and shielding," having weightier results, and unexpectedly gaining an undeserved reputation are perhaps the first major characteristics of the new bin Laden type terrorist organizations. In addition, having learned how to use economic means and taking advantage of the loopholes in the free economics initiated by the West, they set up management-type companies and banks and engage in large-scale drug trafficking and smuggling, the resale of munitions, and the printing of large amounts of forged currency, and rely on the contributions of religious followers to attain stable capital resources. On this basis, the tentacles of these new terrorist organizations extend to even wider areas, and the means are also diversified, such as widely using religious and heretical organizations to develop their own media for propaganda, setting up anti-government militia organizations, etc. The easy accomplishment of raising funds guarantees that they will be able to attain and master large amounts of high technology means so that they will be able to kill even more people with great ease. . . .

Newly converging . . . are the international financial speculators. Although there is still no one listing these immaculately dressed . . . fellows in the ranks of terrorists, yet in terms of their actions and the calamitous consequences they have caused in England, Mexico and Southeast Asia, [no terrorists] can even hold a candle to them. Taking the big financial crocodiles as represented by Soros, on the strength of *a daily business volume exceeding US$120 billion in floating capital, he used financial derivative methods as well as free economic regulations to repeatedly play tricks to foment trouble, so as to bring about one financial upheaval after another. As a result, the area of harmed nations gradually enlarged from Southeast Asia to Russia and then to Japan, and finally to Europe and the United States ... so that the existing world financial system and economic order were fundamentally shaken. . . . The typical characteristics of terrorism including being transnational, concealed, without rules, and tremendously destructive, have given us reason to call this financial terrorism.*

Before the tremendous state apparatus, terrorists and their organizations are perhaps not worth mentioning in terms of numbers of peoples and methods, but in fact there is not one country that dares to look at them lightly. . . . This is a group of maniacs which does not act according to the rules. A terrorist organization which possesses nuclear weapons is definitely much more dangerous than a nation with the same nuclear weapons. The creed of bin Laden is "If I die, then I will also not let others live," and therefore, he would stop at nothing, so that in order to kill ten Americans he would also drench several thousand innocent people in a pool of blood. Soros's logic is "I entered the room to steal money because your door was not locked." In this way, he does not have to be responsible for destroying the economies of other nations and throwing the political order of others into disarray.

For bin Laden who hides under the hills of Islamic fundamentalism, Soros who conceals himself within the forests of free economics, and the computer hackers who hide themselves in the green curtains of networks, no national boundaries exist, and borders are ineffective. . . . They . . . carry out wanton destruction within a regulated sphere and act wildly and run amuck within an unregulated sphere. . . . Perhaps those who check the destruction of rules and those who revise the rules are both necessary. This is because any destruction of rules always brings on new problems which need to be rigorously dealt with. In an age when an old order is about to be removed, those in the lead are frequently those who are the first to destroy the rules or those who are the earliest to adapt to this situation. . . . In this respect, the new terrorists have already walked to the head of the international community.

The most ideal method of operation for dealing with an enemy who pays no regard to the rules is certainly just being able to break through the rules. Recently, in coming to grips with enemies that appear and disappear in the domain of non-military warfare, the Americans have used cruise missiles, Hong Kong has used foreign currency reserves and administrative measures, and the British government has broken conventions so as to allow their secret service organizations to "legally" assassinate the leaders of foreign nations who they consider to be terrorists. This reveals an updating of the rules and a changing of the methods of operation. However, it also reveals . . . dullness in thinking and singleness in method. It is said that the Americans have already decided to employ hacking methods to search for and seal up the bank accounts of bin Laden in various nations, so as to basically cut off his source of capital. This is no doubt a breakthrough in method of operation which goes beyond the military domain. However, we must also say that in this area, the new and old terrorists who consistently uphold the principle of resorting to every conceivable means are still the best teachers of each nation's government.

The colonels make an excellent point about the unintended consequences of international agreements that restrict various types of warfare, including nuclear, chemical, and indiscriminate bombing of civilian population centers. Those kinds of restrictions make warfare harder for any nation that lags behind the United States in precision military technology and, therefore, make unrestricted warfare a much more attractive alternative.

In this section they explicitly link "traditional" terrorists, financial manipulators, and computer hackers under the overall umbrella of unrestricted warfare. All three groups share a disdain for the rules of the international order, and the authors imply that the United States has no moral authority to enforce those rules after we have also repeatedly disregarded them. The more that both strong and weak countries work around global rules imposed by organizations like the UN, the more momentum will build toward total unrestricted warfare. The authors correctly note that unrestricted warfare can do as much or more damage to countries as conventional warfare, just in less obvious ways.

Again, I have to note their prescience in singling out Osama bin Laden, who was ahead of the curve in pursuing financial and communications strategies for terrorism along with more traditional tactics like bombings and assassinations. Bin Laden's ultimate goal wasn't to kill lots of Americans, or even to spread a climate of fear across the country. His real goal was to bankrupt the United States by forcing us into a protracted and crushingly expensive war in the Middle East—and in that sense he succeeded. That's why the CCP saw Al Qaeda as a useful if unwitting partner in China's stealth war to keep America distracted, internally divided by partisan politics, and massively overcommitted to foreign wars.

The key target in this section is the rules-based order itself. The authors are telling the CCP that only suckers and losers follow international rules. Nations that want to rise from the ashes and dominate the world should ignore the UN and its ilk. This willingness to publicly accept rules while privately flaunting them is at the heart of the CCP's effectiveness. They can say things like, "Yes, we will help fight climate change," while deliberately building more coal-fired plants. Because free-world politicians believe that any public commitment will be honored, they pat themselves on the back and act like they've saved the world when China signs something like the Paris Climate Agreement.

But in actuality, a signed treaty is merely a piece of paper. China never wants anyone to go back to check their work, because it would look bad on them. Ever wonder why climate activist Greta Thunberg has never uttered a word about China? She knows the power of portraying America and Europe as the bad guys on climate, because they have responsive political systems that will rein in economic activity if there is enough public outcry. The same cannot be said for China, where the CCP says one thing and does another, and the public isn't allowed to protest.

FLICKING AWAY THE COVER OF THE CLOUDS OF WAR

... To date, the trends of the development of the weaponry of the United States military, the changes in defense policies, the evolution of combat theories ... are all following along quickly on one path. They affirm that military means are the final means for resolving future conflicts,

and the disputes between all nations will ultimately end up with two large armies meeting on the battlefield. Given this premise, the American military is requiring itself to nearly simultaneously win wars in two battle areas, and they have done a great deal of preparation for this. . . .

The age of wars being a matter of moving weapons and soldiers has still not been translated into history, but as a concept it has already begun to noticeably fall behind. Following the increase in the number of international treaties limiting the arms race and the proliferation of weapons, the United Nations and regional international organizations have enlarged their intervention power in local wars and regional conflicts and relatively decreased the military threat to national security. . . . Yet the springing up of large amounts of new high technology will actually greatly increase the possibility of non-military measures threatening national security, and the international community, which is at a loss of what to do upon being confronted with non-military threats. . . . Aside from increasingly intense terrorist attacks, as well as the hacker wars, financial wars, and computer virus wars that will dominate the future, there are also the present various types of "new concept wars" to which it is difficult to fix a name. . . .

American military circles . . . have pushed the resolution of [the nonmilitary problem] *on to the politicians and the Central Intelligence Agency so that they have retreated from the existing . . . non-combatant military operations. . . . They have tightened up more and more so that they have shrunk into a watching tree hung full with various types of sophisticated weapon fruits waiting for . . . an idiotic rabbit to come and knock into it. However, after Saddam knocked himself dizzy at the bottom of this tree, who else is there who would become . . . this rabbit?*

Given their state of mind of "looking around in the dark with daggers drawn," the American soldiers who had lost their opponent due to the collapse of the former Soviet Union are vehemently searching for a reason not to allow themselves to be "unemployed." . . . From the generals to the common soldiers, from the spear of attack to the shield of defense, from major strategies to minor methods of operation, everything that the American military does is in preparation of gaining victory in a major war. . . . The result was that without an enemy, one still had to be created. Therefore, even if it is a tiny area such as Kosovo, they cannot pass up an opportunity to try out their frosty blades. American military circles . . . are now in the realm of forming non-military warfare. This is possibly owing to a lack of sensitivity to new things and also possibly a result of work habit, and even more so possibly due to limitations in thinking. Regardless of the reason, the American soldier always locks his own field of vision in the range covered by war clouds, and this is an indisputable fact.

Even though the United States bears the brunt of the threat of this type of non-military war and has been the injured party time after time, yet what is surprising is that such a large nation unexpectedly does not have a unified strategy and command structure to deal with the threat. . . . They have 49 departments and offices responsible for anti-terrorist activities, but there is very little coordination and cooperation among them. Other nations are not that much better than the United States in this area. . . . [The United States budgets] seven billion dollars for anti-terrorism which is only 1/25 of the US$250 billion military expenditure.

Regardless of how each nation turns a deaf ear to the pressing threat of non-military warfare, this objective fact is encroaching upon mankind one step at a time. . . . People will discover that when mankind focuses more attention on calling for peace and limiting wars, many . . . things in our peaceful lives begin one after another to change into lethal weapons which destroy peace. Even those golden rules and precepts which we have always upheld also begin to reveal a contrary tendency and become a means for some nations to be able to launch attacks against other nations or certain organizations and individuals to do so against society.

[Just as wherever] *there is a computer then there is a computer virus, and when there is currency there is monetary speculation, freedom of faith and religious extremism. . . . It is possible for each field that at any moment tomorrow there will break out a war where different groups of people are fighting at close quarters. The battlefield is next to you and the enemy is on the network. Only there is no smell of gunpowder or odor of blood. However, it is war as before, because it accords with the definition of modern warfare: forcing the enemy to satisfy one's own interests. It is very obvious that none of the soldiers in any one nation possesses sufficient mental preparation against this type of new war which completely goes beyond military space. . . .*

The new threats require new national security views, and new security views then necessitate soldiers who first expand their fields of vision prior to expanding their victories. This is a matter of wiping away the long narrow cloud covering of war cast over one's eyes.

The colonels' diagnosis of America's underfunding of antiterrorism, and the lack of coordination among the Pentagon, the CIA, and other agencies in facing unconventional threats, would be proven tragically accurate after 9/11. One of the most shocking and disturbing lessons from Al Qaeda's successful attacks was how the terrorists were able to exploit the fragmentation of various organizations tasked with protecting our country in different realms. In the age of unrestricted warfare, the clear lines among the military, the intelligence services, federal law enforcement, foreign policy, and regulation of the private sector (including airlines) all blur to the point of vanishing. Twenty years after 9/11, we're still trying to figure out what should replace those clear lines.

In 2020, I was stunned to realize that our medical establishment was also a target. Investigation into the origins of COVID lockdown policies, widespread mandatory use of masks and social distancing, even the oft-incorrect PCR tests all find their origins in the CCP. Among the Western democracies, only Taiwan recognized the CCP's disinformation campaign for what it was. While America and Europe were busy locking down, Taiwan relied on voluntary measures that more resembled the CDC's own recommendations prior to January 2020.

I had traveled to Taiwan in January 2020 to monitor the election process. I attended two huge political rallies in Taipei. Very few people were wearing masks in spite of the fact that Taiwan was already aware of and had started alerting the population to the spreading virus. To this day Taiwan has never instituted mandatory measures for coronavirus, trusting free people to make informed choices.

This also says something about the CCP's brand of modern political warfare. In a world where social media is used to shame nonconformists, the CCP finds it exceedingly simple to manipulate the populations of free countries. Pay experts to write articles highlighting a problem; then get social media to post comments about the article; then use bots to amplify those comments. Eventually, the planted message goes viral and the mainstream media begins to pick up the rallying cry. Before long, anyone who questions the validity or rationality of the message is "canceled" for being unscientific, un-American, or Neanderthal.

What the two PLA colonels realized long before 2020 was that the vaunted U.S. military had become the modern equivalent of the French Maginot Line—giving the appearance of security while leaving the vulnerable underbelly (economic opportunity, social cohesion, and political independence) open for attack. In other words, I trained as a B-2 pilot to wage war far from America's shores while the PLA was waging war on my family's support for our constitutional republic, in my own living room.

If you follow the news in the fall of 2021, it can seem that China is close to being the dominant story: Chinese espionage, threats from Xi Jinping, fear in Taiwan, cyberhacking, Chinese stocks crashing under new government dictates, China and the Taliban, endless questions about the origin of COVID, and more. The activities of the Chinese Communist Party in so many spheres of the world can seem overwhelming. Indeed, they are because they are all part of the plan. A key to unrestricted war, the colonels write in the next chapter, is to be overwhelming. To launch all of your weapons in a blizzard to confuse and demoralize your enemy. The events you're reading about aren't random.

CHAPTER 9

DEPLOYING ALL
OF THE ABOVE

SUN TZU AGAIN PROVIDES SOME RELEVANT WISDOM WHEN it comes to explaining the colonels' emphasis on bringing to bear the many assets of stealth war. And doing it rapidly. "All warfare is based on deception. . . . Let your plans be dark and impenetrable as night, and when you move, fall like a thunderbolt," the great strategist wrote. He advocates using spies and agents to study and demoralize the enemy to the point that when an attack comes, the outcome is decided. "Attack a defeated enemy," he counsels. "The Army is the coup de grace."

He also displays his remarkable sense of restraint and practicality. War should be fought in the shortest possible time with the least cost in lives—and the fewest casualties to the enemy. "No country," he said profoundly in 500 B.C., "has ever benefitted from a protracted war."

In this chapter, his disciples, the PLA colonels, modernize these essential theories of Sun Tzu. The real power, the colonels argue, comes from combining many actions at one time. Flooding an enemy with an onslaught on multiple fronts creates confusion, communications gaps, even fear and panic—and surrender. The tactics of combined arms is not a new military concept. Its origins may well be Chinese, in that it was advocated as far back as *The Art of War.* Centuries later we saw Napoleon orchestrate infantry, artillery, and cavalry in lethal sequence, the Nazis' devastating blitzkrieg of air, armor, and mobile troops overwhelm northern Europe with remarkable speed, and the Americans' use of multiple kinds of combined arms in many campaigns, including the "shock and awe" barrage of high tech and high explosives that stunned Iraq in 2003.

But in *Unrestricted Warfare,* we see an argument for combining military and *nonmilitary* assets. Any and all hostile acts that can be directed at an enemy are fair game. They need to be *added* to the mix in as many ways as possible. Not either/or, but all of the above. In fast or slow motion. But a lot at once. And leading to the same objectives of confusion, fear, and ultimately submission. Also, they are best deployed against an enemy that would have no coordinated defense—because such a defense would be quite complicated to mount, even if you saw the assault coming. The colonels "combination war," then, combines with their earlier key assertion of "no limits war." No limits. Combined war. Not X times 2, but X cubed.

Qiao and Wang stress two points: the combination of "arms" leverages the power of each, and the breadth of their scope overwhelms any defense that is not fully combined to meet the threat in unexpected places. The idea of combination surfaces in several chapters, establishing it as one of their most important insights. Weaker nations need uncommon assets and leverage to confront stronger nations.

Their reading of military history reiterates the power of combination, but finds it contained to only the best military minds. Which leads to a memorable section that brilliantly updates military theory and does so with a tortured analogy that must have been better in the original meaning:

It can be affirmed that whoever is able to mix a tasty and unique cocktail for the future banquet of war will ultimately be able to wear the laurels of success on his own head.

They also make a seminal point that relates back to the idea that their work is one of doctrine, not strategy or policy. They stress that their theory of "combined war that goes beyond limits is first of all a way of thinking, and only afterwards is it a method." Their ultimate goal is to reorient the thinking of the Chinese leadership: the CCP, the generals, and the best students emerging from the best military academies. They want the masters of a second-rate China to envision the many assets—and leverage—they actually possess, even in the face of the seemingly invincible United States, "lord of the mountain." They make a good case.

They again chide the United States for not seeing the evolution of combined war and make an eerie reference to the kinds of problems we might face.

Whether it be the intrusions of hackers, a major explosion at the World Trade Center, or a bombing attack by bin Laden, all of these greatly exceed the frequency band widths understood by the American military. The American military is naturally inadequately prepared to deal with this type of enemy psychologically, ... and especially as regards military thinking and the methods of operation derived from it.

There had been a bombing at the World Trade Center in 1993. But the colonels intuited something more. They were right about our inability to see it coming. It has since been documented that our intelligence and military communities completely missed the rise of Osama bin Laden and his successful plot to fly planes into the World Trade Center and Pentagon. Despite his having enough of a profile for the colonels to take note of him, the U.S. government had no idea where he was and what he was up to.

From Chapter 5 of *Unrestricted Warfare*

COCKTAIL IN THE GREAT MASTER'S CUP

... *When perusing the military history of both East and West, we never find the expression "combination" in any of the descriptions related to methods of operation. However, all the great masters of warfare throughout the ages seem to have instinctively known this principle well....*

General Schwarzkopf who created the miracle of a major battle in which only over one hundred soldiers were lost cannot be considered to be on the great master level.... But ... this commander led a large modern army ... which gave importance to the combination of the important elements of warfare.... The key to driving the Iraqi army out of Kuwait, restoring the life line of oil to the West, and regenerating America's influence in the Middle East, depended on how to ingenuously use the alliance, manipulate the media, use economic blockades, ... along with developing and bringing together various

armed services of the army, navy, air force, space, electronics, etc.
comprised by the militaries of over 30 nations. . . .

The colonels' standard of "master" is quite high, given their ac-
colades for Stormin' Norman. But it was only one campaign and he
had some great talent around him, both up and down the command chain. They are tough critics, and astute about why grand
victories are hard to come by.

Regardless of whether a war was 3,000 years ago or at the end of
the 20th century, it seems that all victories display one common phe-
nomenon: the winner is the one who combined well.

While being able to ever increase the means used for warfare, as
well as make continuous improvements . . . the connotation of this has
also begun to deepen. More factors which had never appeared in the
warfare of the past have entered the world of warfare through the
combination of various different methods. . . .

For the vast majority of soldiers or high-ranking military officers
utilizing the element combination method to carry out warfare is often
an unconscious action. Therefore, their combinations often remain on
the level of weapons, deployment methods and the battlefield, and the
drawn-up war prospects are mostly only limited to the military do-
main. . . . Only those trailblazing military geniuses are able to stand
alone in breaking convention, breaking through limitations and con-
sciously combining all of the means available at the time. . . .

If it is said that combination was only a winning secret formula
of a few geniuses, then consciously making combination the trend . . .
is already becoming clearer day after day, and warfare is now being
taken into an even broader and even more far-reaching domain;

however, all of that provided by the age of technological integration leaves combination with more seemingly infinite possible space. It can be affirmed that whoever is able to mix a tasty and unique cocktail for the future banquet of war will ultimately be able to wear the laurels of success on his own head.

A crucial point: Because military innovators have always experimented with combining new weapons with more established weapons to devise new strategies and tactics, the same will be true with unrestricted warfare, just on a vastly broader canvas. The authors are making the case for an intentional, systematic approach to combining various tactics, rather than experimenting haphazardly or unconsciously.

The tactics they are talking about, however, are not those of the battlefield, but of the boardroom. Public relations, social media, finance, trade, and economics work together in a globalized, internet-connected world to enable limited strikes or massive takedowns. A financial collapse can destroy the capacity of a nation to defend itself just as quickly as a nuclear strike by preventing access to much-needed capital. This can all happen through illicit means to ensure the attacker is not attacked militarily. Systemic failure is the best case scenario, because it is likely that no one will be held accountable. This happens frequently, and thus provides good cover.

We saw this especially in 2020, when the CCP masterfully used the COVID pandemic to destabilize the Western democracies with powerful combinations of unrestricted warfare tactics involving financial, trade, and media disinformation components. China's combination strategy during COVID even included an academic component. Do you remember hearing about a terrifying report in early 2020 that predicted as many as two million American deaths from COVID? That report came from the Imperial College London, which receives millions of dollars in funding from the CCP and has an incentive to align with the CCP's messaging. There are strong signs that the CCP used its influence to induce Western panic, overreaction, and economy-killing restrictions—far beyond what was really necessary to fight the pandemic.

Then they introduce the other element to the combination theory: addition.

USING ADDITION TO WIN THE GAME

... What we have still not spoken of is another term: addition. ...

In a boxing arena, a person who from start to finish uses only one type of boxing method to fight with an opponent is naturally not one who can combine straight punches, jabs, swings and hooks to attack his opponent like a storm. The principle of this can be said to be extremely simple: one plus one is greater than one. The problem is that such a simple principle ... has been surprisingly unclear to many persons responsible for the security and warfare of nations. ...

This has been done from Alexander to Napoleon even up to Schwarzkopf. They do not know that their ability to understand or not understand combinations is not the key to the problem. What is truly important is whether or not one understands what goes with what to implement combinations. ... Lastly ... is whether or not one has thought of combining the battlefield and non-battlefield, warfare and non-warfare, military and non-military which is more specifically combining stealth aircraft and cruise missiles with network killers,

combining nuclear deterrence, financial wars and terrorist attacks,
or simply combining Schwarzkopf + Soros + Xiaomolisi + bin Laden.
This then is our real hand of cards. . . .

Strange to see George Soros and Osama bin Laden in the same
sentence again, but by now the colonels have well established them
as iconic villains, standing in for two types of malevolent force.
Next, they also caution that unrestricted war is not a simple business and must be built on a strong intellectual foundation. It is a
theory based on experience that must be ingested, not a game plan
to be executed.

However, prior to utilizing addition, it must go beyond all of
the fetters of politics, history, culture, and ethics and carry out thor-
ough thought. Without thorough thought, there can be no thorough
revolution.

Before this, even Sun Tzu and Clausewitz locked themselves in the
barrier of the military domain, and only Machiavelli approached the
realm of this thought. For a very long period of time, . . . the thought of
the Prince and its author were both way ahead of their time, [and]
were held in contempt by the knights or rulers. They would naturally
not be able to understand that going beyond all limits and boundaries
was an ideological revolution, which included the premise of a revo-
lution of military thought. In the same way, to date, those who only
understand an imposing array of troops on the battlefield and who
think that war is just killing people and methods of operation are just
methods to kill people and that there is nothing worth giving attention
to other than this, have been unable to understand this point. . . .

When "a military gives excessive focus on dealing with a specified type of enemy," this can possibly result in their being attacked and defeated by another enemy outside of their field of vision. Steven Maizi and Thomas Kaiweite [of the Strategic Studies Institute of the U.S. Army War College] *correctly expressed their concerns about this. They further pointed out that "Even though official documents stress the army . . . it is necessary to break through fixed modern Western thinking to broaden the conception of future conflicts. However, most of the descriptions of how the digitized troops of the 21st century will conduct war sound like an armored war using new technology to fight with the Warsaw Pact nations." . . . Such ridiculous wishful thinking can only bring one type of future prospect: "The vast majority of development plans of the present American military . . . are all focused upon dealing with an enemy with conventional heavy armor, and if the United States encounters an enemy with low level technology, an intermediate level enemy, or one with equivalent power at the beginning of the next century, then the problem of insufficient frequency band width will possibly occur."*

Actually, with the next century having still not yet arrived, the American military has already encountered trouble from insufficient frequency band width brought on by the three above mentioned types of enemies. Whether it be the intrusions of hackers, a major explosion at the World Trade Center, or a bombing attack by bin Laden, all of these greatly exceed the frequency band widths understood by the American military. The U.S. is inadequately prepared to deal with this type of enemy psychologically, and especially as regards military thinking and the methods of operation derived from this. This is because they have never taken into consideration and have even refused to consider means that are contrary to tradition and measures of operation other than military means. This will naturally not allow them to add and combine the two into new measures and new methods of operation. In actuality, it only requires broadening one's outlook a little and being uninhibited in thought to be able to avail oneself of the lever of the great volumes of new technology and new factors springing up from the age of integrated technology....

It would be well if we were somewhat bold and completely mixed up the cards in our hand, combined them again, and saw what the result would be.

Supposing a war broke out between two developed nations already possessing full information technology, and relying upon traditional methods of operation, the attacking side would generally employ the modes of great depth, wide front, high strength, and three-dimensionality to launch a campaign assault against the enemy. Their method does not go beyond satellite reconnaissance, electronic countermeasures, large-scale air attacks plus precision attacks, ground outflanking, amphibious landings, air drops behind enemy lines.... The result is not that the enemy nation proclaims defeat, but rather one returns with one's own spears and feathers. However, by using the combination method, a completely different scenario ... can occur. If the attacking side secretly musters large amounts of capital without the enemy nation being aware of this at all and launches a sneak attack against its financial markets, [and] *then after causing a financial crisis buries a computer virus ... in the opponent's computer system ... while at the same time carrying out a network attack against the enemy so that the civilian electricity network, traffic dispatching network, financial transaction network, telephone commu-*

nications network, and mass media network are completely paralyzed, this will cause the enemy nation to fall into social panic, street riots, and a political crisis. There is finally the forceful bearing down by the army, and military means are used . . . until the enemy is forced to sign a dishonorable peace treaty. This admittedly does not reach the domain spoken of by Sun Zi [Sun Tzu], wherein "the other army is subdued without fighting." However, it can be considered to be "subduing the other army through clever operations." It is very clear who was superior and who inferior when comparing these two methods of operation. . . .

Based on this thought, we need only shake the kaleidoscope of addition to combine into an inexhaustible variety of methods of operation.

In this section the authors are getting more specific about the power of combining various kinds of unrestricted warfare with the operations of traditional warfare, in particular directed at the weaknesses of the United States. The possibilities for new combinations are infinite—and infinitely terrifying.

The ultimate example is again 2020, when the CCP deployed trade warfare against the Trump administration and a sophisticated disinformation campaign about coronavirus at the same time. During the beginning of the pandemic, the CCP locked down supplies like personal protective equipment (PPE) and masks inside China and through proxy companies outside. Overnight, China became a net importer of these items, when they had previously been a net exporter. The CCP even talked about taking advantage of the spreading pandemic by leveraging the world's need to use Chinese manufacturing to solve their pandemic-related supply chains problems.

Price gouging flourished even while the CCP was using "mask diplomacy" to advertise the Chinese model of economic, political, and social control by the CCP as the best way to combat the coronavirus. It became a triumphant narrative of Communist-system success over democracy frequently lauded by U.S. media in 2020.

Meanwhile, domestic air travel was locked down in China beginning in late January while international travel continued into March. As the virus spread through Europe and other areas, the WHO was repeating the CCP narrative that calling the virus anything but COVID-19 was xenophobic and racist. Today we have a UK variant and a South Africa variant with no media accusations of bias or xenophobia for using those terms. The combinations and additions are subtle and almost invisible, unless you know what to look for.

THE MIRACULOUS EFFECTS OF
ADDITION AND COMBINATION

Any type ... of method of operation can be combined with another ... to form a completely new method of operation. Regardless of whether it is intentional or unintentional, the carrying out of combined methods of operation using different methods of operation that go beyond domains and categories has already been applied by many nations in the practice of warfare. For example, the countermeasure used by the Americans against bin Laden is national terrorist warfare + intelligence warfare + financial warfare + network warfare + regulatory warfare. Another example is what the NATO nations used to deal with the Southern Alliance Kosovo crisis: deterrence with the use of force + diplomatic warfare (alliance) + regulatory warfare. Prior to this, the

United Nations under pressure mainly from the United States adopted the methods of operation against Iraq: conventional warfare + diplomatic warfare + sanction warfare + media warfare + psychological warfare + intelligence warfare. We also noticed the means adopted by the Hong Kong government . . . in August of 1998 to deal with financial speculators were: financial warfare + regulatory warfare + psychological warfare + media warfare, and even though they paid a heavy price, the results of the war were very good. . . .

We can see from these examples the miraculous effects of applying addition-combination in methods of operation. If it is said that, owing to the limitations of technical measures and conditions, those engaged in warfare in the past were still unable to freely combine all factors for winning wars, then today the great explosion of technology led by information technology has already provided us with this type of possibility. Only if we are willing and do not allow subjective intentions to depart from objective laws, will we then be able to arrange the cards in our hand . . . based on need, until finally winning the entire game.

Yue Fei, the military strategist during the Song Dynasty in China, stated when discussing how to employ methods of operation that "the subtle excellence of application lies in one-mindedness." Although this statement sounds very abstruse, yet it is actually the only accurate explanation of the correct application of combination. . . . This is then having the myriad methods converge into one. . . . Aside from combining the transcendence of being unfettered, you have no way of imagining what other method of operation can transcend the net of combination. The conclusion is thus so simple, and yet it will definitely not arise from a simple brain.

"One-mindedness," an ancient concept, speaks to the kind of co-ordination that the modern Chinese Communist Party has brought to its ongoing decades of stealth war. In many places, the colonels stress the need for high-level command and control over the multiple forms of warfare they have articulated. Conversely, they chide the United States for its inability to even conceive of this need. It is remarkable that the CCP seems to have been so successful at maintaining this coordination and discipline for so long. They are not invincible, as I will explain in the next chapter, but the capabilities they have displayed make them a formidable enemy.

TEN THOUSAND METHODS COMBINED AS ONE

On May 7, 2021, unidentified hackers penetrated the computer networks of Colonial Pipeline, the company that operates a vital 5,500-mile artery of gasoline, diesel, and jet fuel between Houston and New York City. The attack was made via ransomware—a form of malware that encrypts data until the victim pays dearly to unlock its own systems. The hackers threatened to release all of Colonial's proprietary data online unless they were paid 75 bitcoin, with a value of just under $5 million. In response, Colonial "pre-emptively shut down its pipeline operations to keep the ransomware from spreading and because it had no way to bill customers with its business and accounting networks offline."* Just like that, a key part of

---

*Nicole Perlroth, "Colonial Pipeline Paid 75 Bitcoin, or Roughly $5 Million, to Hackers," *New York Times,* May 13, 2021, https://www.nytimes.com/2021/05/13/technology/colonial-pipeline-ransom.html.

the energy supply chain to thirteen states in the southeast and mid-Atlantic was paralyzed.

The hack "triggered a cascading crisis that led to emergency meetings at the White House, a jump in gas prices, panic buying at the gas pumps, and forced some airlines to make fuel stops on long-haul flights, as the *Times* story said. Shortages triggered a rush to stock up on gasoline in the affected states, which quickly made the shortages even worse. In many locations, drivers waiting in hours-long lines got into screaming fights over access to the rapidly emptying gas pumps. With seemingly no option to solve the crisis after a six-day shutdown, Colonial paid its extortionists the nearly $5 million, receiving in return software that slowly began to unlock its systems. But fully restoring pipeline operations took weeks; as late as May 18, more than ten thousand gas stations were still depleted.

The ransomware attack shocked many observers who had never realized how vulnerable our aging energy infrastructure would be to cyberthreats. Investigations soon suggested that the mostly likely culprit was DarkSide, a shadowy Eastern European cybercriminal group that may or may not have ties to the Russian government. But many questions remain unanswered. We may never know if this attack was simply motivated by financial extortion, or if geopolitical goals also played a part.

The PLA colonels who wrote *Unrestricted Warfare* would say that it ultimately doesn't matter if the hack was orchestrated by greedy criminals, a dissident political faction, or Vladimir Putin himself. Any of them can now comfortably hide behind a veneer of anonymity.

America is far more undefended than most of its citizens can imagine—vulnerable to a nearly infinite range of attacks that the colonels predicted more than two decades ago. Just imagine the chaos and suffering if a future Colonial-style hack was combined with separate, simultaneous hacks against our electricity grids, air traffic control, and financial markets.

The colonels were thinking this way when they introduced Chapter 7 of *UW* with a quote from the futurist Alvin Toffler: "Today's wars will affect the price of gasoline in pipelines, the price of food in supermarkets, and the price of securities on the stock exchange. They will also disrupt the ecological balance and push their way into every one of our homes by way of the television screen." Toffler was right; we just need to add the smartphone and social media to make his point contemporary for the 2020s.

By this point in *UW,* the colonels have shattered the reader's traditional definition of war as something that happens on the well-defined battlefields of land, sea, and air. They've made an undeniable case that future wars may include every aspect of life that Toffler mentioned, along with many more. And we're still not even close to prepared.

The U.S. military used technology to fight anonymity in Iraq in the 2000s when we set up a process for analyzing DNA found on improvised explosive devices. These data were loaded into a biometrics database so that the evidence could be used to plan raids on bomb-making hideouts. That was a step in the right direction, but we haven't kept up. Adversaries ranging from the CCP to DarkSide have gotten very good at protecting their anonymity via the blockchain, cybercurrency, and other dark aspects of the internet.

Cyberwarriors can attack literally anywhere from anywhere, and the PLA hides safely behind China's Great Firewall as it launches attacks around the world.

The colonels note that five centuries ago, Machiavelli had a clearer sense of unrestricted warfare than most modern military or civilian leaders. Perhaps Americans would be better prepared for our stealth war with China if every officer candidate was required to read Machiavelli (or at least *Unrestricted Warfare*) rather than Clausewitz.

From Chapter 7 of *Unrestricted Warfare*

THE WAR BEYOND THE BATTLEFIELD

Most of the warriors will be inadequately prepared or will feel as though they are in the dark: the war will be fought and won in a war beyond the battlefield. . . . A chasm has already appeared between traditional soldiers and what we call modern soldiers. . . . The [necessary new] method is to create a complete military Machiavelli.

Achieve objectives by fair means or foul, that is the most important spiritual legacy of this Italian political thinker of the Renaissance. . . . It meant using means, some possibly comprehensive, without restraint to achieve an objective; this holds for warfare also. Even though Machiavelli was not the earliest source of "an ideology of going beyond limits" (China's Han Feizi preceded him), he was its clearest exponent. . . .

In terms of war, this could mean [erasing] the boundary between the battlefield and what is not the battlefield, between what is a weapon and what is not, between soldier and noncombatant, between state and non-state or supra-state. Possibly it might also include technical, scientific, theoretical, psychological, ethical, traditional, customary, and other sorts of boundaries. In summary, it means all boundaries which restrict warfare to within a specified range. . . .

In past wars, the combination of weapons, means, battle arrays, and stratagems was all done within the limits of the military sphere. This narrow sense of the concept of combinations is, of course, very inadequate for today. He who wants to win today's wars, or those of tomorrow, . . . must "combine" all of the resources of war which he has at his disposal and use them as means to prosecute the war. . . . [This] is the concept of "going beyond limits," surpassing all boundaries and conforming with the laws of victory when conducting warfare with combinations. . . .

This gap between the traditional and modern mindsets was a big reason why I retired from the Air Force a few years ago. I could see that the people in charge of America's military either weren't willing or weren't able to comprehend how they had been out-flanked by unrestricted warfare, and how it was making the Pentagon less and less effective in defending the country.

I was trained to fly a B-2 up to 6,000 miles to drop bombs on an enemy's military targets. But, meanwhile, many of the young recruits who were refueling my plane or loading its bombs no longer really believed in the Constitution or democracy, in large part because of China's systematic interference in our media, social media, politics, and economy. I realized that if we didn't reverse this trend soon, the sophistication of our aircraft and the skill of our pilots would become irrelevant; we would collectively lose sight of the nation's priorities and lose the will to defend them. I realized that I could better serve my country by sounding the alarm from outside the military.

Up to now, most people involved in warfare considered all the non-military domains . . . as accessories to serve military needs. The narrowness of their field of vision and their way of thinking restricted the development of the battlefield and changes in strategy and tactics. From . . . the massive bombing of Dresden and the nuclear destruction of Hiroshima and Nagasaki, inflicting countless civilian casualties in the pursuit of absolute military victory, to the strategic propositions of "massive retaliation" and "mutually assured destruction," none of these broke this mold. . . . The great fusion of technologies is now impelling the domains of politics, economics, the military, culture, diplomacy, and religion to overlap each other. . . . Add to this the influence of human rights consciousness on the morality of warfare. All of these things are rendering more and more obsolete the idea of confining warfare to the military domain and of using the number of casualties to measure the intensity of a war. Warfare is now escaping from the boundaries of bloody massacre, and exhibiting a trend towards low casualties, or even none at all, and yet high intensity. This is information warfare, financial warfare, trade warfare, and other entirely new forms of war. . . .

On October 19, 1987, U.S. Navy ships attacked an Iranian oil drilling platform in the Persian Gulf. News of this . . . immediately set off the worst stock market crash in the history of Wall Street. This event, which came to be known as "Black Monday," caused the loss of $560 billion in book value to the stock market. . . . In the years since then, time after time, military actions have touched off stock disasters which *then led to economic panic. . . . If one intentionally takes two or more mutually unconcerned domains and combines them into a kind of tactic one can use, isn't the result better?*

Every American officer in every branch is taught the law of armed conflict, which includes the importance of distinguishing between combatants and civilians, applying proportionality in responses, and doing one's best to spare civilian property from collateral damage. These international principles were developed in response to the World War II incidents that the colonels mention here, as well as to the postwar doctrine of mutually assured destruction as a deterrent to catastrophic nuclear war.

For career officers like me, hearing that there are actually no rules, no restrictions against using any kind of force, is extremely hard to swallow. So is the idea that the traditionally rigid walls among different domains of the U.S. government—especially the Defense Department, the State Department, the Treasury Department, and the Federal Reserve—need to become flexible or collapse entirely. It will take a fundamental mindset shift for the leaders of all those domains to grasp that we can win an unrestricted war only if they coordinate their powers and set aside their instinct to protect their autonomy.

Furthermore, in this "war without rules" environment, we must acknowledge the emergence of new domains. One widely discussed example was the Reddit discussion group r/wallstreetbets, which coordinated lots of small investors whose enthusiasm for GameStop stock forced powerful hedge funds to cover their short positions. The big guys on Wall Street lost billions while the little guys on Reddit scored outsized profits, at least in the short term.

Millions took up day trading via free platforms like Robinhood, with minimal capital required.

Now imagine this army of Reddit-directed small investors being subtly manipulated by a foreign power to buy or sell stocks that would have a strategic impact on our economy. That's exactly what China's 50 Cent Army has already done effectively with propaganda posts on Facebook and other social media to influence our elections and policies. For all we know, they might have already anonymously expanded into Reddit, Robinhood, and other platforms that can wreck our stock market—just as effectively as that 1987 military incident triggered Black Monday.

Even more challenging: This kind of mayhem can happen in broad daylight, without any warning. Traditionally, during any international crisis our intelligence community looks for indicators of an attack in order to provide the Department of Defense with fair warning. But internet-driven stealth attacks during peacetime conditions can go completely unanticipated and undetected. America's intelligence apparatus cannot peer into the domestic internet, making it impossible to detect and defend against these types of attacks.

As we've discussed, the coronavirus was a prime example of an act of unrestricted, undeclared warfare. The international medical establishment, which is responsible for warning the world about any potential pandemic, starts from the assumption that all nations will be truthful about a potentially catastrophic disease. In December 2019, Taiwan's CDC got wind of a new strain of pneumonia in Wuhan and sent investigators to ask questions. They couldn't get clear answers because the CCP was obfuscating. The investigators

returned to Taiwan, warned the WHO, and immediately implemented measures to protect the Taiwanese people. (Not lockdowns,
which the United States would later implement at the urging of
the CCP and WHO, but voluntary precautions like those in the
American CDC's playbook.)

If the U.S. intelligence community had been attuned to potential acts of unrestricted warfare, they would have been better prepared to alert our authorities to what was happening and ignore
China's false reassurances. Then the United States could have
warned the rest of the free world, which could have jointly blocked
all travel to and from China before it was too late. Instead, we allowed international travel to continue to avoid the appearance of
racism, exactly as the CCP hoped.

SUPRA-MEANS COMBINATIONS

*During a war between two countries, during the fighting and killing
by two armies, is it necessary to use special means to wage psychological war aimed at soldiers' families far back in the rear area? When
protecting a country's financial security, can assassination be used
to deal with financial speculators? Can "surgical" strikes be made
without a declaration of war against areas which are sources of drugs
or other smuggled goods? Can special funds be set up to exert greater
influence on another country's government and legislature through
lobbying? And could buying or gaining control of stocks be used to
turn another country's newspapers and television stations into the
tools of media warfare?*

[These are all what we call] *"supra-means combinations."* . . .

Although economic assistance, trade sanctions, diplomatic mediation, cultural infiltration, media propaganda, formulating and applying international rules, using United Nations resolutions, etc., belong to different domains such as politics, economics, or diplomacy, states-men use them more and more now as standard military means. . . .

During the crisis in 1979 when Iran occupied the U.S. Embassy and took hostages, at first, all the U.S. thought of was the rash use of military means. Only after these failed did it change tactics, first freezing Iran's foreign assets, then imposing an arms embargo, and supporting Iraq in the war with Iran. Then it added diplomatic nego-tiations. When all these channels were used together, the crisis finally came to an end. This shows clearly that in a world of unprecedented complexity . . . a better means used alone will have no advantage over several means used in combination. Thus, supra-means combinations are becoming extremely necessary. It's a pity that not many countries are aware of this. On the contrary, it is those non-state organizations in pursuit of various interests which are sparing no effort in the use of means in combination. For example, the Russian mafia combines assassination, kidnapping for ransom, and hacker attacks against the electronic systems of banks in order to get rich. Some terrorist organizations pursue political objectives by combining means such as throwing bombs, taking hostages, and making raids on networks. . . . The likes of Soros combine speculation in currency markets, stock markets, and futures markets. Also they exploit public opinion and create widespread momentum to lure and assemble the "jumbos" such as Merrill Lynch, Fidelity, and Morgan Stanley . . . to join forces in the marketplace on a huge scale and wage hair-raising financial wars one after the other. . . .

If some economically powerful company wants to attack another country's economy while simultaneously attacking its defenses, it cannot rely completely on the use of ready-made means such as economic blockades and trade sanctions, or military threats and arms embargoes. Instead, it must adjust its own financial strategy, use currency revaluation or devaluation as primary, and combine means such as getting the upper hand in public opinion and changing the rules sufficiently to make financial turbulence and economic crisis appear in the targeted country or area. . . . Even a quasi-world power like China already has the power to jolt the world economy just by changing its own economic policies. If China were a selfish country, and had gone back on its word in 1998 and let the Renminbi lose value, no doubt this would have added to the misfortunes of the economies of Asia. It would also have induced a cataclysm in the world's capital markets, with the result that even the world's number one debtor nation, a country which relies on the inflow of foreign capital to support its economic prosperity, the United States, would definitely have suffered heavy economic losses. Such an outcome would certainly be better than a military strike. . . .

The use of means singly will produce less and less effect. The advantages of the combined use of various kinds of means will become more and more evident.

Since *UW* was published, America's annual defense budget has grown to nearly $800 billion, yet we're more vulnerable than ever to much poorer adversaries who are using the types of combined means described in this section. In particular, the rhetorical question about using psychological warfare against the families of soldiers is very real in the age of social media. While pilots like me are striking targets on the other side of the world, our families are very likely reading antiwar, anti-American propaganda planted by our adversaries on Facebook, Twitter, or TikTok. If skillfully constructed, this propaganda goes viral because Americans willingly share it without investigating its origins or accuracy.

"If China were a selfish country . . ." is pretty funny in this context. China under the CCP was already extremely selfish during the 1998 Southeast Asian financial crisis. It used that crisis to engineer a new banking system that would be impervious to attack. By establishing a nonconvertible currency and strict capital controls while simultaneously becoming the world's biggest producer of physical goods (including everything from Air Jordans to iPhones), the CCP could ensure a steady supply of incoming cash against a tightly controlled flow of outgoing cash—because companies like Nike and Apple can't convert their currency at will. This gives the CCP regime ample resources to finance its goals.

While pretending on the surface that China is the innocent victim of the United States, the colonels are (between the lines) urging the CCP to become even more ruthless in its quest for global hegemony.

The authors wrap up their chapter by stressing the importance of blue-sky brainstorming about unrestricted combinations at all levels of conflict, from big picture strategy to the most granular tactical details. The sky, for them, is truly the limit.

SUPRA-TIER COMBINATIONS

. . . The trend of warfare shows more and more clearly . . . : it is definitely not the case that problems at one level can only be solved by means at

the same level. No matter whether it is allocating only a fraction of the resources, or using a big machete to kill a chicken, it is a feasible method so long as it works well.

Bin Laden used a tactical level method of only two truckloads of explosives and threatened U.S. national interests on the strategic level, whereas the Americans can only achieve the strategic objective of protecting their own safety by carrying out tactical level retaliation against him. Another example is that in past wars, the smallest combat element was the combination of a man and a machine, and its usefulness would normally not go beyond the scale of battles. In beyond-limits war, by contrast, the man-machine combination performs multiple offensive functions which span the levels from battles to war policy. One hacker + one modem causes an enemy damage and losses almost equal to those of a war.

They were wrong about Osama bin Laden in one sense: He was never tied to the 1993 World Trade Center bombing. But some of his later accomplices were responsible, and their "two truckloads of explosives" were only a prelude to what Al Qaeda would later accomplish with just nineteen jihadists.

CHAPTER 10

CALLING IT WAR

IN 1998, THE PER CAPITA GROSS DOMESTIC PRODUCT OF CHINA was about $800 billion—in range of places like India and Pakistan. That same national income for the United States was about forty times higher, around $33,000 per person. The U.S. military was the dominant force in the world with a huge blue water navy, thousands of deployed troops in Asia, the most sophisticated air force in the history of man. A new age of technology was pumping supercomputers and personal computers out of Silicon Valley. Wall Street banks were financing global growth and printing profits. Communism was a dead ideology, on life support in a few mausoleums like Cuba. But Colonels Qiao and Wang were not deterred.

Where others might have seen their homeland as a bloated, lumbering nation permanently relegated to second-world status, they saw opportunity. Their book ends with a rallying cry, a pep talk for Chinese leaders. They amplify their case that the world has changed in ways that provide lowly China with great opportunities—language used twenty years later by Xi Jinping.

The Peace of Westphalia, that centuries-old bedrock premise of civility which strove with ultimate success to stop the endless bloodshed of European nations, was now extinct. The new world would be one without rules. And China, for all its historical burdens, was primed to win. If only the leadership would agree to wage a new kind of war, one with no restrictions. The language in the finale is stirring, and ought to be the basis for a rallying cry of our own.

But before the colonels get to the crescendo, they lay out their theories in the form of a military-style doctrine. They fold their key theories into concise militaryspeak, and as such they are not all revolutionary. Their eight keys to "beyond-limits combined war" include terms found in many other military manuals: "omnidirectionality," "synchrony," and "asymmetry." They make a few good points but often drift into dense language and contradictory advice. It's not the sort of warfighting strategy you could put on an index card and keep in your pocket.

I suspect they felt the need to play to their military audience in a conventional way, after having laid out a very unconventional plan. Many Chinese leaders had been closely studying the U.S. military since the first Gulf War, but always from a military perspective, such as weapons systems, force deployments, and tactics. Perhaps the colonels thought their total war idea so revolutionary that the manual needed a dose of conventional wisdom. Regardless, it was the revolutionary doctrine that took hold as the book became widely read among the CCP leadership and in the academies training the next generation of political and military cadres.

As they work toward a conclusion, the colonels are trying to consolidate their theories into a workable doctrine that can be taught and applied. They want to refashion basic military principles to their new way of war. They succeed in part. Here's how they lay it out:

From Chapter 8 of *Unrestricted Warfare*

OMNIDIRECTIONALITY—*360 DEGREE* OBSERVATION AND DESIGN, COMBINED USE OF ALL RELATED FACTORS

. . . In terms of beyond-limits warfare, there is no longer any distinction between what is or is not the battlefield. Spaces in nature including the ground, the seas, the air, and outer space are battlefields, but social spaces such as the military, politics, economics, culture, and the psyche are also battlefields. And the technological space linking these two great spaces is even more so the battlefield. . . . Warfare can be military, or it can be quasi-military, or it can be non-military. It can use violence, or it can be nonviolent. It can be a confrontation between professional soldiers, or one between newly emerging forces consisting primarily of ordinary people or experts. . . .

This seals their point that the weapons of war involve all aspects of national power, "supra-national combat power," as they call it. The next key is about managing this plethora of weaponry in a coordinated and timely fashion for maximum impact.

SYNCHRONY—CONDUCTING ACTIONS IN DIFFERENT SPACES WITHIN THE SAME PERIOD OF TIME

The technical measures employed in modern warfare, and in particular the spread of information technology; the emergence of long-range warfare technology; the increased ability to transform the battlefield; the linking together of battlefields which stretch forever . . . and the introduction of various military and non-military forces on an equal footing into the war—all these things greatly shrink the course of warfare. So many objectives which in the past had to be accomplished in stages through an accumulation of battles and campaigns, may now be accomplished quickly under conditions of simultaneous occurrence. . . . Thus, stress on "synchrony" in combat operations now exceeds the stress on "phasing."

Beyond-limits war brings key factors . . . to bear . . . executing a well-arranged team-effort and combined attack to achieve surprise, secrecy, and effectiveness. A single full-depth, synchronized action . . . may be enough to decide the outcome of an entire war. . . .

This closely mirrors the concept of information-driven network-centric warfare first proposed by Vice Admiral Arthur Cebrowski and John Garstka during a military review ordered by President George W. Bush. But the colonels envision applying the concept across the breadth of national power.

The next two keys are intriguingly related and echo some of the historical Chinese cautions about the need for restraint. The colonels stress the difference between "limited objectives" and "unlimited measures." In other words, pick your goal with care, don't overreach—but then throw everything you have at that goal. At one point they offer what they call a "bit of Eastern wisdom": "Going beyond the limit is as bad as falling short."

This has the feel of the Powell Doctrine. Again, however, Colin Powell was referring to the conventional notion of warfare as opposed to the steady state of peace. The two colonels do not differentiate. To them, China is always at war and must be poised to seize opportunities as they arise. There is no better example of this than the Communist leaders' manipulation of the COVID virus outbreak.

LIMITED OBJECTIVES—SET A COMPASS TO GUIDE ACTION WITHIN AN ACCEPTABLE RANGE FOR THE MEASURES

... When setting objectives, give full consideration to the feasibility of accomplishing them. Do not pursue objectives which are unlimited in time and space.... [This] *will only lead to disastrous consequences....*

Mistakes committed by the Americans in Vietnam and the Soviets in Afghanistan ... prove that no matter what sort of action it is and no matter who is executing it, when objectives are greater than measures, then defeat is certain....

UNLIMITED MEASURES—THE TREND IS TOWARD UNRESTRICTED EMPLOYMENT OF MEASURES, BUT RESTRICTED TO THE ACCOMPLISHMENT OF LIMITED OBJECTIVES

... Unlimited measures to accomplish limited objectives is the ultimate boundary....

The employment of unrestricted measures can only be, as Confucius put it, "as one pleases, but not beyond the rules." Here, "rules" means objectives. . . . A smart general does not make his measures limited because his objectives are limited.

Sherman's advance toward Savanna in the American war between the north and south was not in search of combat, it was to burn and plunder all along the way. It was a measure used to destroy the economy in the southern army's rear area, to make the southern populace and the southern army lose the ability to resist, thus accomplishing the north's war objective. This is an example of the successful use of unlimited measures to achieve a limited objective. . . .

They have little original to say about asymmetric war, a strategy that has been a problem for the United States and other large powers since the early days of post–World War II insurgent movements such as Vietnam. They talk of exploiting an enemy's "soft spots" and refusing "to confront the armed forces of the strong country head-to-head." But it is a relevant reminder that tactics such as surprise attacks can be just as potent when using nonmilitary force.

ASYMMETRY—SEEK NODES OF ACTION IN THE OPPOSITE DIRECTION FROM THE CONTOURS OF THE BALANCE OF SYMMETRY

. . . Mostly the weaker side selects as its main axis of battle those areas or battlelines where its adversary does not expect to be hit. The center of mass of the assault is always a place which will result in a huge

psychological shock to the adversary. . . . It often makes an adversary which uses conventional forces . . . look like a big elephant charging into a china shop. . . .

The colonels' concept of "Minimal Consumption—Use the Least Amount of Combat Resources Sufficient to Accomplish the Object" is pretty much incomprehensible. To the extent it makes a point, it contradicts the notion of deploying unlimited measures at limited goals. Another key, "Adjustment and Control of the Entire Process," makes the obvious point that because this multilayered attack will move quickly and rely on vast quantities of data, it needs to be managed with much more sophistication. More important is their recommendation for "Multidimensional Coordination," which lays out very clearly the need for the military to take charge of civilian actors. One can see Xi Jinping's program of civil-military fusion as conforming to this line of thinking.

MULTIDIMENSIONAL COORDINATION— COORDINATING AND ALLOCATING ALL THE FORCES WHICH CAN BE MOBILIZED IN THE MILITARY AND NON-MILITARY SPHERES COVERING AN OBJECTIVE

. . . On the face of it, this definition is not at all novel. Similar explanations are to be found in many combat regulations, both obsolete and newly published. The only difference between it and similar explanations is, and this is a great difference, the introduction of non-military and non-war factors into the sphere of war directly rather than indirectly. In other words, since any sphere can become a battlefield, and any

*force can be used under combat conditions, we should be more in-
clined to understand multidimensional coordination as the coordination of the military dimension with various other dimensions in
pursuit of a specific objective.*

The colonels end their doctrine section with succinct and cautionary advice:

*All of the above principles are applicable to any beyond-limits
combined war.*

*Victory is certainly not in the bag just because a side adheres to
the above principles, but violating them no doubt leads to defeat.
Principles are always essential conditions for victory in war, but they
are not the only conditions.*

*In the absence of a principle that victory is certain, there are only
essential principles. We should always remember this point.*

Their brief concluding chapter describes a world disrupted
and makes the case for an upstart nation to take advantage. They
make a final plea to the CCP to exploit the enormous opportunity
in front of them. They express confidence that China can overtake
the United States as the world's leading superpower, despite how
daunting that challenge must have seemed in 1999.

For all their discussion of unconventional war, they lament that
violent war is also not going away. "Mankind's dream of peace is still
as elusive as ever. Even speaking optimistically, war will not be wiped
out rapidly within the foreseeable future, whether it is bloody or not."
Given that reality, the task for China is simple: "What we can and
must focus on at present is how to achieve victory."

From the Conclusion of *Unrestricted Warfare*

... The modern concept of "nation states" which emerged from the Peace of Westphalia in 1648 is no longer the sole representative occupying the top position in social, political, economic and cultural organizations. The emergence of large numbers of meta-national, trans-national, and non-national organizations, along with the inherent contradictions between one nation and another, are presenting an unprecedented challenge to national authority, national interests, and national will....

Although the boundaries between soldiers and non-soldiers have now been broken down, and the chasm between warfare and non-warfare nearly filled up, globalization has made all the tough problems interconnected and interlocking, and we must find a key for that. The key ... must be suited to all the levels and dimensions, from war policy, strategy, and operational techniques to tactics; and it must also fit the hands of individuals, from politicians and generals to common soldiers.

We can think of no other more appropriate key than "unrestricted warfare."

As I read those words again twenty years after first encountering them, they took on a whole new meaning. This was not the fantasy conclusion of a couple of obscure military thinkers. This was a detailed mission statement for national revival. The tone is coldly clinical and direct. Like good soldiers, they avoid hyperbole. But they display a sort of genius for describing a clear plan that draws on Chinese history, current party thinking, and future opportunities. At the moment when America's power seemed at its height, they saw vulnerabilities and drew a map to exploit them. My colleagues in the military community and I found it unrealistic and somewhat bizarre. China was making plans to defeat the United States? But there was nothing bizarre about the book's reception in Beijing.

Now I get it. The actions prove the theory. In so many of the ways that I laid out earlier, the CCP has followed the manual. When I published *Stealth War* two years ago, I detailed a series of actions by the Chinese that sought unfair advantages in science, trade, and other businesses. But I felt that many of these events were one-off incursions that might have been explained by other factors. I was aware of *Unrestricted Warfare*, but had not studied it in detail. That deeper read has led me to see that there are no one-offs in our contacts with China. Everything is part of a grand strategy, and everything is part of a long-term war.

To be sure, there are other keys to understanding the CCP's plans. I'm not suggesting *Unrestricted Warfare* is Xi Jinping's bible consulted daily. Even Western military doctrine cautions against dogma. We have occasionally seen other books, studies, and speeches that make similar points about America as the enemy and asymmetric war as the answer. But in my view none is as clear as *UW*. I started this book by talking about the two most recent Chinese outrages: the Hong Kong takeover and the evil manipulation of the COVID pandemic. Both incorporate so many elements from the colonels' text: information control and deception through technology; swift, coordinated movements; co-opting international organizations; disdain for the rule of law; lashing out at criticism from

Australia with immediate trade sanctions. Both were, at least in the short run, victories for China. And victories that did not involve firing a shot. I would add, however, that they also might violate the colonels' rule about limiting one's objectives. A major consideration going forward is whether the CCP has overplayed its hand, and whether this might have created an exploitable weakness. On the other hand, we might have just witnessed a dry run for the takeover of Taiwan.

That China has weaknesses needs to be part of our discussion, both so we are not intimidated by their power and, equally important, so we can formulate a more realistic counterattack. We have to start by accepting that the United States has never confronted anything quite like modern China. In little more than a generation, China transformed from a destitute agrarian society to a significantly wealthy country with a large and growing middle class, an unimaginably large population, and a growing impact on the world. The United States has become tied to China in innumerable ways, mostly having to do with the products China makes and that we buy— because we allowed so much of our manufacturing to move there.

The average Chinese citizen takes pride in these accomplishments, and with good reason. As I've said, I admire the Chinese people and wish for the day when they are not ruled by a totalitarian dictatorship. But I'm also concerned that this national narrative—from victim to victor—creates a lot of political support for Xi Jinping and his megalomania. I particularly worry about the military, where generations of PLA officers have been trained to strive for Chinese redemption and greatness. Redemption from the centuries of humiliation by the Western powers, and greatness to be achieved at their expense. There are analogies that can be taken from both Imperial Japan and Weimar Germany in the decades before World War II. In both places, wounded national pride, a need for resources and land, and a powerful military establishment created an inexorable drive toward war. China may well be on the same path, particularly as it applies to Taiwan.

There is no question that the leaders of the CCP see the world through an exactly opposite lens from the United States and Western-style democracies. They do not believe in freedom, democracy, and the rule of law. They don't believe in the free flow of information or capital. They believe that totalitarian government is the best form for controlling mankind, they support dictators with similar views, and they work to bring more nations along that path. They want to create "a community of common destiny for mankind," as Xi Jinping reminds us constantly. Of course, this happens only through the work of the CCP, and in alignment with their interests. Thus the number one goal of the Chinese Communist Party is the survival of the party. And their number one enemy has to be the United States.

But China also has long-standing and self-inflicted problems. It has an aging populace, a shrinking workforce, an increasingly government-controlled economy, a fragile monetary system plagued by huge debt, and world opinion that might have finally caught up to its deceits and human rights abuses. It has been so deft at extracting talent, technology, and capital from the West that it has managed to hide those vulnerabilities in a cloak of invincibility.

While China is on track to become the world's largest economy in the next decade, that is in total gross domestic product rather than per capita, which is far below that of the United States. The CCP crows about its bright new middle class—maybe 300 million to 400 million people—but that leaves another billion who are not well off. An estimated 600 million people live on $150 per month. And that's assuming we trust their numbers.

Thanks to their insane one-child policy, China's productive workforce might have peaked already. The predominance of males causes social problems. The country's racist and isolationist culture makes immigrating workers implausible, unless they are enslaving their own Uyghur minority Muslims. China has to know that its manufacturing supremacy is in trouble. Therefore, the Belt and Road Initiative is their path to redemption. They need the populations and resources of member countries to preserve their power, and the power of those who rule similarly in member states.

The government is imposing even more control over what was already a command economy. Overbuilding of real estate and infrastructure—the gleaming, empty buildings they like to show off—has created mountains of debt that many analysts think are bubbling up to a financial crisis. In one of the CCP's strangest moves, in 2021 they began clamping down on their most successful companies and entrepreneurs, perhaps fearing that they were becoming independent power centers that thrived on free market principles. Now expanding are the many giant and inefficient state companies, intent on defying the history of failure for similar enterprises around the world.

Politically, the CCP—and really President Xi Jinping—is also reverting to more control rather than more freedom. Xi aims to become the new Mao, moving to name himself president for life.

History's lessons of the dangers of myopic one-man rule have been lost.

China's neighborhood is not compliant. It is bordered by or near strong countries—Japan, South Korea, Taiwan, India, Australia among them—that do not want to see it dominate Asia. More immediately, they don't want the South China Sea to become a Chinese lake. Or for Taiwan to go the way of Hong Kong. Yet at the same time their companies are incentivized to see their economies inextricably linked to China's extractive future growth model.

Also significant is that public sentiment in the rest of the world might have woken up to the fraudulence of the "Chinese Miracle." Many countries besides the United States cheered the coming of China into the family of man. And, of course, profited from it. Optimists saw a do-good and do-well scenario for the developed world. Poor China now had a place at the table and would civilize, said Western countries, and our companies could make a lot of money in the process. The cheating and stealing of technology and markets and competing enterprises were ignored as the World Trade Organization and other entities opened their arms and welcomed the new kid on the block. Now, they're starting to think the kid might be a sociopath. Consider the facts: the incomprehensible Uyghur genocide—declared such by the U.S. State Department; the mindless ongoing repression of Tibetans; the grotesque violation of treaties—and common sense—in the repressive takeover of Hong Kong; the insidious refusal to help the world with the COVID crisis that they themselves had created. The accumulation of all this cannot be a one-off. This is criminal behavior. And the average citizen of the world is waking up to that reality. We'll have to wait and see about their governments, given the enormous amount of corporate pressure to keep playing what the capitalists naively consider to be China's game.

But my most important concern: Has the government in Washington turned?

By "government" I mean the White House and the concentric circles, both official and unofficial, that emanate from cabinet departments, congressional committees, think tanks, the media, and other places of influence. Making, and changing, policy comes through a many-layered sieve in Washington. It's often slow and stumbling. But sometimes there is clarity and consensus. I hope this is one of those moments. And I believe the facts in this book can help build that consensus.

By now you know my point: China is at WAR with the United States. We don't realize it yet. We need to. And then we need to radically change our policy to deal with that reality.

It's not a shooting war, as our friends Colonel Wang and Colonel Qiao make clear. But it is modern, comprehensive, and effective.

While people say hindsight is 20/20, the colonels had 20/20 foresight in predicting the shift toward using nonmilitary means to undermine and slowly strangle democracies around the world. It might be understandable that our China experts didn't grasp the implications of *UW* in 1999, but it's unforgivable that so many government officials today still don't grasp what the CCP is doing. I've found that to be true in my conversations with senior people in all corners of Washington.

Many of us have been conditioned to assume that nations abide by international laws and treaties that they've willingly signed, and we find it hard to contemplate that a head of state's signature might be worthless. We need an entirely new lens to view an emerging superpower that has no interest in honesty, integrity, law, or justice—only in expanding its power by any means necessary.

The Chinese Communist Party understands that it holds the high ground when it comes to these new battlefields. In fact, a few years ago Premier Li Keqiang bragged about China's superior access to data in a meeting with President Trump. Because China has no laws preventing the government from spying on its citizens, the CCP is free to spy on everybody, everywhere. This allows them to collect massive amounts of data to improve their artificial intelligence. Unless we can compete aggressively in the development of AI, China and other authoritarian powers will have a massive advantage, because of their unrestricted access to data.

The colonels stress the need to change a nation's ideology and mindset before it can fully embrace unrestricted warfare across previously separate domains—military, financial, cultural, diplomatic, and so on. For leaders who have spent their lives thinking of these domains as distinct and governed by their own rules and principles, this mindset shift can be extremely difficult, if not impossible.

For instance, while it may seem a stretch to connect the Black Lives Matter movement to the CCP, that social issue offered precisely the type of American vulnerability that China is eager to exploit. During the first meeting between the CCP and the Biden administration in 2021, top diplomat Yang Jiechi criticized the United States by citing BLM protests: "Many people within the United States actually have little confidence in the democracy of the United States." This kind of false-equivalence attack blunts our efforts to criticize China's widespread human rights abuses.

Racism is also frequently invoked to deflect criticism of the CCP. For example, when China was criticized for enabling the spread of the coronavirus in early 2020, the CCP claimed that this accusation was not merely false but was a racist attack on Chinese people worldwide. This was classic projection, because the CCP is itself a racist organization that has been accused of literal genocide against the Uyghurs of East Turkestan, which the CCP forcibly annexed in 1949 after the Chinese Civil War. The world has done far too little to stop the ethnic cleansing of the Uyghurs.

The colonels predicted that globalization and the internet would enable China to exploit the openness of free societies and their willingness to give ideologies like Marxism a fair hearing in the marketplace of ideas. Sure enough, our university system and social media have become major avenues of attack—breeding grounds where Western self-censorship would gain a following. The trendy ideology of "cancel culture" sprang from Marxism and was thus ripe for exploitation by the CCP as Americans and citizens of other free societies have become increasingly afraid of blowing up their careers by saying something deemed offensive.

Before long, as we saw earlier, even actors and sports stars like John Cena and LeBron James felt they had to apologize to the Chinese people for disagreeing with the CCP's positions on Taiwan, Hong Kong, the Uyghurs, or any other issue. If they had resisted, the damage to their global careers would have been too great to bear. These public acts of deference deflect critiques of the CCP's regime—including within China itself, where the government can proudly announce that even famous people from the Western democracies agree with the CCP. Pressuring famous people to self-censor is a very effective weapon in the propaganda war.

Thanks to President Trump and some of the visionary people around him, the Washington consensus on China has moved in a more confrontational direction. But I don't think far enough. My former colleagues at the National Security Council pushed for and got some significant restraints on Chinese behavior, including restricting trade, blocking companies with military ties from accessing U.S. investor capital, and protecting U.S. telecommunications networks from Chinese software. The administration of President Biden has so far continued those policies and there is even bipartisan consensus on Capitol Hill to get tougher.

Yet almost all the discussion of how to deal with China centers on words like "engagement" and "management." China is viewed as a "challenge" or a "competitor," as if we needed to gear up for another round of World Cup soccer. There have been many words expended on China from the best think tanks and analysts who are read by the policy makers. Most of them well meaning. And most of them wrong. Couple that with the fact that there are significant players outside government who don't want to acknowledge China's aggression, conveniently couching it as routine competition from a budding superpower. Those folks are the ones profiting from China—mainly companies in Silicon Valley and Wall Street—and one would be naive to underestimate their power.

I remain optimistic about America's ability to confront China's unrestricted warfare and to counterattack with some unrestricted tactics of our own. My goal in this book has been to warn you that we have to change our mindset about what constitutes war and how it is fought—but also to reassure you that it's not too late. We still have massive advantages in our economy, technology, and military that make the United States a beacon of hope and liberty around the world. There are many specific actions we can take, as I outline in the next chapter. We just need to summon the will to do what's necessary to live up to our highest and noblest principles.

That starts with a clear and honest assessment of the hostility we are facing. We need to see the China threat as a war. And respond as we would to war. It's not a "challenge" or a "competition" or a situation to be "managed."

War is war. The colonels just told us so.

So what do we do about it? I have some ideas.

CHAPTER 11

FIGHTING BACK
WITH NEW RULES

THINK ABOUT HOW THE COVID PLAGUE MIGHT HAVE BEEN different if we had viewed the Chinese Communist Party as a hostile opponent. Just speculate on how much better it would have been if China was honest with the United States and the world—as if that was ever going to happen. But if we were paying attention to the lessons of *Unrestricted Warfare*, we would have known to be suspicious and even distrustful of their comments on the emergence of an unusual disease. Before it started, of course, we would have taken very seriously the reports from our embassy that there were safety problems with the Wuhan labs. We would have been aware and monitoring at a high level the presence of Chinese military in those labs. We would not have funded the work of those labs. Upon early reports of an outbreak, we would have greatly restricted travel to the region and begun checking Chinese passengers for symptoms. We would not have let China play such a dominating role in the World Health Organization and would likely have been able to get better advice to the rest of the world. Past viruses have been controlled. It's hard to speculate if this one could have been, but assuming the worst from China and trying to contain it as their problem could have saved many lives.

China's lies and manipulation should make all Americans ready to understand the China threat. And, I hope, take action. Because while confronting China head-on is not a simple matter for our government, it can involve some simple actions by ordinary citizens and voters. What you buy, how you invest your money, and whom you vote for can be powerful weapons in stopping Chinese aggression.

The goal is to stop China's destructive actions now, then to cause their government to reform and join the law-abiding community. That's going to take macrolevel strategic changes by our government, but also microlevel actions by individuals, businesses, and other civic institutions.

We need a defense to meet an offensive we're only beginning to understand: beyond-limits combined war. China is a formidable enemy for a Cold War, a giant nation that is deeply embedded in the American economy. Unlike the Soviet Union, which produced nothing we wanted, China has become our factory floor for everything from toys to cell phones. Through their theft, they are becoming competitive in the most high-tech areas such as supercomputing and artificial intelligence. They have a space program and a rapidly growing military. And they very suddenly have developed an arsenal of nuclear missiles that might match those of our own and of the Russians.

But they are not invincible. We need to take some of the wisdom we've gleaned from the colonels who wrote *Unrestricted Warfare* and turn it back on their masters. China has a range of economic and social problems that can be exploited. For instance, their economy is more fragile than it appears. They are betting on an inflexible system of government and one-man rule that never works. They have dropped their camouflage of "hiding and biding," but their blatant aggression has turned world opinion against them.

"What is of supreme importance in war is to attack the enemy's strategy," Sun Tzu advocates. Now we know their strategy. And we know the principles they have followed to execute that strategy:

- Know the face of war. It is combined, unrestricted war that seeks victory through nonviolent means, but does not rule out violence.
- Know your enemy, his strengths and weaknesses.
- Join your forces to meet the threat; create "one-mindedness." Focusing the many parts of our government on the single objective of stopping China is essential.
- The people must be in harmony with their leaders.

We have begun to understand some of these principles and act on them. As I write this in the fall of 2021, the Biden administration has continued most of the assertive policies of the Trump era. Many members of Congress are pushing a pile of bills to stop China on issues such as technology theft and slave labor. The new Chinese ambassador, one of the so-called wolf warrior diplomats, had no sooner arrived in Washington than he gave an angry speech warning the United States of "disastrous consequences" if we sought to counter China with a "Cold War playbook." That told me we were making progress. But not enough. The Trump policies were a breakthrough but fell short because they were not widely coordinated throughout the government, they were sold too harshly as punishment, and they became politicized as did most things involving Donald Trump. That they stayed in place testifies to their validity. Now we need to move on to the next steps.

We need to map out a positive, globally inclusive strategy built on three pillars: Protect, Rebuild, and Inspire. China's actions are both a threat and an opportunity. We have to remember that the Chinese seek to impose an exact opposite form of government on the world. The opportunity is to revitalize the framework that has improved so many lives. Attack their strategy.

These three pillars are intended to reshape the international order away from totalitarianism and toward the promotion of human rights, democracy, civil liberty, rule of law, and economic prosperity. Exploitation of labor and environmental challenges are also confronted as global supply chains reorient to nations that support competitive markets, strong labor protections, and environmental standards.

Protect

Building on the idea of trade with democratic nations that support our values, we must continue tariffs and other protective mechanisms, such as the Foreign Investment Risk Review Modernization Act (FIRRMA). This pillar seeks to refine and export tools that incentivize those nations that play by the rules of fair and open markets to tighten collaboration in economic, financial, trade, and information flows. This involves reducing the ability of rule breakers to use U.S. allied and partner nations to exploit the free system's near-open borders to avoid tariff and other protections.

Make tariffs permanent for the CCP-led Chinese economy and contingent on an annual vote in Congress, which considers whether China is a human rights violator and if it has a market-based economy. Replace the Wassenaar Arrangement of voluntary export controls with an enforceable economic alliance that seeks to ban the transfer of technology and capital to totalitarian or authoritarian nations that disavow free trade, democratic principles, rule of law, and self-determination. Build a robust and resilient locally based military communications system (C4ISR: command, control, communications, computers, intelligence, surveillance, and reconnaissance) for the Indo-Pacific to decrease the attractiveness of Chinese targeting of U.S. space-based assets. Shift defense procurement away from legacy weapons systems to those favoring intermediate-range ballistic and cruise missiles based in the first island chain, and hypersonic equivalents based in Alaska.

On finances, direct the Department of Labor to allow every person in this country who participates in a public or private pension fund to opt out of sending their investment dollars to China, and to designate that a portion of their funds be invested in manufacturing in their local communities. Use the purchasing power of the federal government to ensure all contracts require only U.S.- and ally-built technology be used. Ensure that foreign companies and countries that access Western capital markets for investment and debt adhere to the same generally accepted accounting principles (GAAP), audit, and transparency standards of domestic companies.

Rebuild

Using President Eisenhower's preference for military deterrence, this pillar involves a massive movement in fiscal spending away from guns toward butter. By focusing on infrastructure, our industrial base, energy, STEM education, and research and development, the United States will rebuild its core economic and science and technological superiority to lead the world once again.

Shift $100 billion from the defense budget to a massive R&D and reindustrialization effort focused on quantum computing, artificial intelligence, machine learning, 5G and telecommunications, the internet of things, nuclear and carbon-free energy, data science, cryptocurrency, biopharma, robotics, logistics, manufacturing, and transportation. Protect these investments with a robust counterintelligence program designed to ensure the benefits of these investments accrue only to America and her allies and partners. Use the national security authority of the president to allocate the sub-6GHz spectrum to any companies willing to build secure and survivable 5G telecommunications and computational infrastructure with no back doors based on identity management, encryption, and access control, and share it with democratic allies and partners. Create a private infrastructure bank for America modeled on the Federal Home Loan Banks system. Commit to a 120-day federal infrastructure project-approval process for any project with a private investment commitment exceeding $50 million—all denials must be approved by the president. Commit $25 billion of the defense budget to STEM scholarships for American students in U.S. universities.

Inspire

Americans are builders not breakers. Leveraging the incredible legacy of the post–World War II Marshall Plan in Western Europe, America will join with developed allies and partners to create a strategic economic development plan that seeks to promote collective economic prosperity tied to democratic principles and rule of law.

Countering China should spur us to forge a new consensus with a global network of allied nations, along with their private sector companies, that collectively seeks to grow promising developing nations that agree to adhere to the principles of free trade, human rights, rule of law, and self-determination. Unite the U.S. International Development Finance Corporation, Export-Import Bank, U.S. Trade and Development Agency, Millennium Challenge Corporation, and the U.S. Agency for International Development under one director, the head of the Office of Strategic International Economic Development. This organization would work with like-minded developed nations to identify and promote the economic prosperity and institutional integrity of like-minded developing partners. Consolidate Foreign Military Sales, International Military Education and Training, Foreign Military Financing policy, strategy, and approval authority under a director of Strategic Military Investment who also would also serve as the deputy director of the Office of Strategic International Economic Development.

Develop a Global Fund for Democratic Infrastructure Investment, which would seek to analyze the global trading routes and infrastructure to invest in a robust, resilient international logistics architecture, which would promote free trade, secure and verifiable customs procedures, and the collective economic prosperity of like-minded nations. Develop an international data-tracking system to clearly show where America, allied nations, and their companies are investing to help smaller companies and institutional investors take advantage of the accompanying economic growth prospects. Bring back the U.S. Information Agency to lead U.S. public diplomacy.

Properly executed, this strategic plan would result in economic growth of greater than 5 percent by tapping into the lowest energy costs, corporate tax rates, massive deregulation, and widespread opportunity zones currently available in the United States and other democratic-friendly markets. By linking a resurging economic and science and technological powerhouse with democratic-allied and partner nations, the United States will forge a new consensus, which will begin to drive positive outcomes in international institutions like the UN and WTO. Together, this coalition of free nations with strengthened economic, financial, trade, and informational ties, buttressed with a robust military alliance focused on deterrence, will fuel a rebound in the growth of democracy around the globe.

There are many specific actions that extend from those strategic concepts, covering all aspects of American society. They have been discussed by a variety of experts, and some have been implemented, some are on the books but without teeth. None has been thought through as part of an integrated strategy directed at a formidable opponent. These are some of the most important:

Political

We need a single coherent team that manages our opposition. It cannot reside in twenty agencies. China comes at us as one force; we need to be one force to oppose them. Ultimately this has to come from the White House, but needs buy-in from the rest of the government.

Economic

Just forcing the Chinese to play by the rules of the global economy will cause a shock. They have been getting away with so much for so long. I mentioned things like accounting rules and stock market requirements. There are thousands of details that an empowered Department of the Treasury or Securities and Exchange Commission could enforce. Congress has been aggressive about proposing new restrictions, such as requiring companies to certify that there is not forced labor in their supply chain.

I don't know if the corporate sector will come along willingly. Even though it is not in their long-term interest to promote a country that defies free markets and the rule of law, the short-term incentives are powerful. Legislation changing that incentive structure is going to be necessary.

We need to see our own growth strategy as a matter of national security. We need to reshore—that is, bring back to the United States manufacturing that we lost. As one example, we should revive government incentives to build a robust domestic semiconductor industry. Those tiny chips have become the engine of technology to the point that society may well not function without them. Future generations of chips will be even more important, and the United States should own the secure supply chain. The world's biggest semiconductor manufacturer today? Taiwan.

We should shadow and look for opportunities to counter the Belt and Road Initiative. China uses its excessive loans to developing countries to gain political leverage. In some cases, countries that have defaulted have been forced to give China long-term access to mineral resources or port access. Working with the World Bank and other nations, we can counter that economic colonialism.

Diplomatic

The Quadrilateral Security Dialogue (Quad alliance: United States, Japan, Australia, India) is a strong deterrent to Chinese aggression. It can be strengthened and expanded. As large as China's military might is, when combined with the United States, the nations of Asia, including South Korea and Vietnam, are more than a match. The AUKUS (Australia, UK, United States) agreement was an incredibly important step in linking the United States, the UK, and Australia beyond a mere military alliance. The sale of nuclear subs to the Australians is an action the Chinese colonels should admire, if grudgingly. While it is an arms sale, it has the added benefit of drawing a line in the sand declaring that China's actions will be countered. This has the additional effect of forcing allies who have been closely aligned economically with China to choose sides. The democratic alliance countering China does not now include countries such as Germany or especially France, given their angst. However, granted that they will not feel comfortable having the PLA defend their interests in Asia like the U.S. military currently does, this will eventually bring them over to the right side.

On climate change, China's blithe disregard of its emissions must be repeatedly called out. They are the world's number one polluter, with their coal-fueled economy emitting almost 30 percent of greenhouse gases—which is double that of the United States'—and climbing. Amazingly, while that fact should make them a pariah, they have managed to turn the issue around to gain leverage over the United States. In the Obama years, many Chinese predations were ignored because we didn't want to discourage them from cutting emissions—which, of course, they have no intention of doing even though they are choking their own country. Growth is all that matters to the CCP. Yet they have continued to dangle the sacred carrot of climate in front of the Biden team and other gullible international bodies.

With China suddenly in possession of nearly as many nuclear weapons as the United States and Russia, where is the outcry for a new weapons treaty? Just because the Chinese are likely to scoff at the suggestion, this is another case where they deserve to be called out so the world can see what it's dealing with.

They have to be challenged in all international bodies. As we've seen, they have co-opted places like the World Health Organization and the World Trade Organization. If we are truly to be on a Cold War footing, the answer is not to quit those bodies, but to aggressively confront and call out Chinese actions and work with allies and partners to deny CCP candidates the leadership of these organizations.

Information

The Chinese Communist Party's clever use of what the colonels call "information warfare" has been one of its greatest successes. It needs to be challenged in the best way we know how: by telling the truth. The basic Chinese narrative is the rise of the East and the decline of the West. From their diplomats to a literal army of paid civilians, that theme is repeated in every form of media. We need to fortify outlets like the Voice of America and Radio Free Asia to tell honest stories about what's really going on in the United States and China. The Great Firewall that blocks ordinary Chinese from the global internet can be breached.

United States–based social media companies need to be encouraged to do a better job of countering Chinese propaganda. Facebook, Google, Twitter, and others say they are committed to publishing accurate information. The constant flood of Chinese falsehoods, intended to create political dissension, should fall well outside their guidelines. Legislation passed in the early days of the internet has held social media companies blameless for what others publish on their sites. But irresponsible behavior can force that to change. And they know it.

In more sophisticated realms, we need to protect the next generation of data. For instance, one key step the United States should pursue is universal encryption. By ensuring that all data in a free society are encrypted and by developing platforms that allow for safe processing of encrypted data, the West can effectively compete with the CCP in artificial intelligence. Fully homomorphic encryption enables analysis of encrypted data so that researchers can solve complex problems without endangering the privacy or data sovereignty of private citizens. That way, our AI can be continually upgraded without providing the type of influence and power that the CCP seeks.

Education

There is great value in Chinese students' coming to the United States to study, but the system has been abused and needs to be tightened. The point is to encourage the Chinese to learn our values and way of life, but not to let them steal our technology. We have leverage here because China does not have the capacity or quality of schools to educate the hundreds of thousands of top students that emerge from its secondary education system each year. American universities earn billions of dollars by admitting them. They need to do a better job of vetting who is allowed in, and the federal government probably needs to help. That said, these Chinese students cannot have access to any Chinese apps like WeChat in the United States. Those are censored and curated by the CCP. They need to be speaking English, using U.S.-based social media, and having the CCP's controlling links broken. Otherwise, they will be here doing the CCP's bidding without truly understanding or appreciating democracy.

Related to this is the growing number of academic espionage cases involving professors and grad students stealing intellectual property. Our counterespionage efforts have improved, but I suspect there is much more that can be done.

Military

One of the hardest questions is how we deal with an expanding Chinese military. While the colonels never envisioned a military that could confront the United States directly, that day is nearing. On the other hand, the theory of *Unrestricted Warfare* is that military expansion is just a ruse to provoke even greater spending by rivals. Starting with their second-rate aircraft carriers and the proliferation of missile silos that may or may not hold nuclear warheads, the Chinese army may be more Potemkin than not.

That said, I do believe the CCP will make a move on Taiwan soon. That means we will have the Pacific equivalent of the Berlin Airlift. We need to be ready to evacuate and resupply the people of Taiwan as well as be prepared to destroy their high-tech manufacturing capabilities for computer chips.

And, of course, the perpetual question is one of intentions. Are China's ambitions confined to Asia? The Belt and Road extends well beyond. Would China use its military in an aggressive manner against its neighbors? The violent skirmishes with India over the disputed Himalayan territory are ominous. And China has other territorial disputes, none more imminent than Taiwan. But if you trust *UW,* their last option would be a military invasion of the island, given that they have so many nonmilitary options at their disposal. How to deal with a kinetic war with China is going to have to be a topic for another book.

Consumers

The solution to the China threat can't just be about politicians and policy. All Americans need to understand that we are indeed at war with China. Do you want to make your enemy stronger? Be skeptical of the products they make and the stories they tell. Don't support evil behavior. Opposing their human rights violations is not just the moral thing to do; it is one of our weapons against them. Boycott Chinese products. Stop shopping at stores that refuse to carry American or democracy-friendly alternatives. We have to give up our addiction to cheap goods. We can pay a little more and buy a little less as long as the products come from the United States or reputable countries.

The ruthless strategy of *Unrestricted Warfare* should make clear that the Chinese Communist leaders are not running a humane nation and, until they reform, must be treated as the outsiders they once were. Chinese citizens should get the message that unless that happens, they will suffer the economic consequences. China may be the world's biggest manufacturer, but the United States is the biggest market for their products.

Don't invest in Chinese companies. Tell your investment adviser to sell any China-related stocks. Certainly, you can do that as a way to send a message. But you can also do it as part of a good investment strategy. Given what we've learned about how they hide their data and succumb to government pressure, I think Chinese companies are bad bets and are going to get worse. Most ridiculous are the companies that portray themselves as part of the ESG (environmental, social, corporate governance) fad—so-called environmentally conscious. China is the least eco-friendly, sustainable place on Earth.

Voters

We should all be China hawks. Power in America comes from the ballot box. Supporting China over the United States should now be seen as unpatriotic. Candidates should have a tough China policy— and not just at the federal level. Governors have made all kinds of deals with China where the benefits flow mostly one way. Those days need to end. Hold your congressperson's feet to the fire. Chinese actions should be presumed guilty of damaging the United States until proven innocent. Support initiatives that diminish the power of parties to dictate the candidate's actions once in office—ranked choice voting and open primaries are such initiatives. This is often exploited by the CCP for its own interests by pressuring corporations to pressure the politicians.

What Does Victory Look Like?

Asked about his strategy to confront the Soviet Union, Ronald Reagan said: "We win, they lose." It was simple, but not simplistic. And it worked. This time it's not so simple. Confronting China raises many complications and dangers. We have so many mutual inter-actions that any changes resemble pulling wood pieces from a tow-ering Jenga pile. But it doesn't have to be a zero-sum game. Our objective is not necessarily to bring China to its knees; it's to force China to stand down from its unrestricted war and to behave like a responsible nation. China—meaning the Chinese people—has so much talent and capacity to make the world a better place. They are a far more important resource to the world than the Soviet Union ever was. But they *have* to be made to play fair.

Make no mistake, this is the challenge of our generation. This is the Clash of Civilizations. When political scientist Samuel Hun-tington wrote his influential book of that title in the early 1990s, he foresaw the rise of China as perhaps the biggest threat to the West-ern world. He thought the power of culture would cause nations with similar ethnic characteristics, such as South Korea and Viet-nam, to accede to China as the regional power. He predicted the "Sinic civilization" would follow a Confucian model of hierarchi-cal society—with China as the hegemon—as opposed to the then-prevailing individual freedoms valued by Western culture. The truth is the CCP's Marxist-Leninist totalitarianism goes beyond Confu-cius, but with no less hegemonic intent. China's neighbors are so far resisting, but they can't do it alone. A stable, safe Pacific region is in everyone's interest.

We have to keep telling the story of what China is currently becoming. Here is the alternative to democracy that they want to impose on the world: a totalitarian hell in which a tiny cadre of party leaders lords over millions of serfs who have no freedom and must show unending loyalty to the government deity. War is permanent. Truth is relative. Man is expendable. To the current leaders of the Chinese Communist Party, George Orwell's dystopic world of *1984* is a guidebook, not a warning. We should thank Colonels Qiao and Wang for helping us understand this alternative future. Now, it's up to us to make sure it doesn't happen.

Seeing this as a monumental clash of ideologies is the main reason that while we can learn from *Unrestricted Warfare*—know your enemy—we cannot wage our own version of it. In some areas, yes. But matching the comprehensive government response, the discipline, and the iron-fisted nature of what the Chinese are doing would ruin our liberal democratic system—something the CCP desires. Instead, it requires a strategy of overt, transparent defense. To invoke the CCP's vulnerabilities, the Chinese must be cut off from the technology, talent, and capital of free societies. There are plenty of ways to do that and still adhere to our values. To still play fair.

We first have to understand the nature of the war being waged against us. And then we need to have the will to win. We have a great country and the China threat should spur us to make it better. The only ones who can beat us are ourselves.

AFTERWORD

WHEN I THINK BACK TO THE FRUSTRATING ARGUMENTS I had about the China threat during my days at the Pentagon and the White House, I'm encouraged to see that just recently our government, and others around the world, may be coming to a consensus about the intentions of the Chinese Communist Party. After decades of ignoring China's destructive behavior, many parts of the U.S. government see it as a danger to our national security. I hope this book will help crystallize that thinking.

As the book goes to press, one of the most encouraging developments came from the CIA, where Director William Burns announced a reorganization to focus more intently on China. He said in a breakthrough statement in October 2021, that "an increasingly adversarial Chinese government" was "the most important geopolitical threat we face in the 21st century."* At the same time, the

---

*Julian E. Barnes, "C.I.A. Reorganization to Place New Focus on China," *New York Times*, October 7, 2021, https://www.nytimes.com/2021/10/07/us/politics/cia-reorganization-china .html.

White House and State and Defense departments have been speaking with one voice about China's belligerence toward Taiwan. A procession of naval exercises has backed up the rhetoric. This sort of coordinated approach was something I pushed for many years. Ironically, it's right out of the colonels' playbook.

Another of my causes at the White House was the vulnerability of our national communications networks to hacking, spying, and sabotage. I particularly argued against the malign influence of the Huawei telecommunications firm—and it probably cost me my job. With backing from Chinese intelligence, the company was intent on dominating the global market for cell phones and transmission sources—in the process creating an endless opportunity for China to eavesdrop on governments and businesses everywhere. But recent bipartisan efforts in Washington, London, and elsewhere saw through that scheme and stopped it. At the moment, Huawei seems in decline and the case against it can be a model to stop other dangerous Chinese enterprises.

I've also decided to do my part to combat information warfare. Realizing how vulnerable our civilian and military infrastructure is to disruption by weapons such as an electromagnetic pulse, I've started a company called SEMPRE, which makes and markets secure cell phone towers and the computing platform to support them. We provide military-grade security for governments, businesses, and individuals. It's a way to prevent hacking, ransomware, and other cybercrimes. As we know, cybercrimes will only grow in volume and increasingly become supported by government sponsors, such as China's United Front army of hackers. Hardening our infrastructure is one of the essential tasks we face.

On the financial front, government agencies are toughening the rules on Chinese companies, forcing them to report honest numbers and play by the rules of global business. Trade officials have so far resisted pressure from the business community to ease the Trump-imposed tariffs that have stalled China's efforts to disrupt our markets. That pressure will only grow as the lure of profits from Chinese trade—as shortsighted as it is—will cause Wall Street bankers and multiple industries to lobby lawmakers to ease up.

And then there is what's happening within China's own borders, giving us a clearer picture of China's weaknesses—but also raising puzzling questions about their intentions. I have always thought that the state-controlled Communist economy can't sustain itself in the long run, and we may be seeing the beginning of that unraveling. The collapse of China's overheated real estate sector could cost trillions in lost savings and disrupt the state-owned banks. Chronic energy shortages are causing blackouts and crippling industrial production. This will exacerbate long-standing woes such as food insecurity and a fast-aging population. Xi Jinping's crackdown on successful companies, notably in the technology sector, is sure to hobble productivity and innovation.

If we're looking, we've just learned a lot about our enemy. Now we have to take advantage of it.

ACKNOWLEDGMENTS

War Without Rules could not have been written without Brian Kelly. His insight and experience made clear the vision we had for this book; I am in his debt. Bria Sandford likewise had the foresight to see the need for this book, at this time. She used her incredible talent to organize complex ideas into a story. Finally, I could not have worked on this project without the dedicated and talented team at SEMPRE, who kept the bytes flowing while I thought about grand strategy.